CHRISTIAN CLASSICS IN
MODERN ENGLISH

Christian Classics in Modern English

Practicing the Presence of God
Brother Lawrence
retold by David Winter

The Imitation of Christ
Thomas à Kempis
retold by Bernard Bangley

The Confessions of St. Augustine
St. Augustine
retold by David Winter

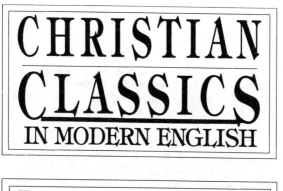

CHRISTIAN CLASSICS
IN MODERN ENGLISH

Practicing the Presence of God
BROTHER LAWRENCE

The Imitation of Christ
THOMAS À KEMPIS

The Confessions of St. Augustine
ST. AUGUSTINE

Harold Shaw Publishers
Wheaton, Illinois

The retelling of **Practicing the Presence of God** was first published as *Closer Than a Brother*, originally published as *Laurie, the Happy Man*, © 1971 by David Winter (London: Hodder & Stoughton). Harold Shaw Publishers' first edition © 1971, this edition © 1991 by David Winter. Published by special arrangement with Hodder & Stoughton.

The retelling of **The Imitation of Christ** was first published as *Growing in His Image*, first edition © 1983, this edition © 1991 by Bernard Bangley. Unless otherwise noted, Scripture quotations are from the *Holy Bible, New International Version*. Copyright © 1973, 1978, 1984 International Bible Society. Used by permission of Zondervan Publishing House. All rights reserved.

The retelling of **The Confessions of St. Augustine** was first published as *Walking into Light*, first edition © 1986, this edition © 1991 by David Winter.

Printed in the United States of America

ISBN 0-87788-121-9

Library of Congress Cataloging-in-Publication Data

Christian classics in modern English.
p.   cm.
    Contents: Closer than a brother : a reinterpretation of Brother Lawrence's Practicing the presence of God / by David Winter — Growing in His image : a reinterpretation of Thomas à Kempis's The imitation of Christ / by Bernard Bangley — Walking into light : a reinterpretation of St. Augustine's The confessions of St. Augustine / by David Winter.
    ISBN 0-87788-121-9
    1. Christian life—Catholic authors. 2. Meditations. 3. Augustine, Saint, Bishop of Hippo. 4. Christian saints—Algeria-Hippo—Biography. 5. Hippo (Algeria)—Biography. 6. Christina life—1960- I. Winter, David Brian. Closer than a brother. 1991. II. Bangley, Bernard, 1935- Growing in His image. 1991. III. Winter, David Brian. Walking into light. 1991.
BX2349.C47   1991
242—dc20   91-25306
                                                                    CIP

99 98 97 96 95 94 93

10 9 8 7 6 5 4 3 2

Contents

THE IMITATION OF CHRIST

THE CONFESSIONS OF ST. AUGUSTINE

Practicing the Presence of God

Brother Lawrence

retold by David Winter

Introduction

Nicholas Herman was born in 1611 in France, of humble parents. He had an experience of conversion at the age of eighteen, and after some years as a soldier and then as a footman, entered a lay community of Carmelites at Paris, where he took the name Brother Lawrence. He died at the age of eighty in 1691.

During the twenty-five years he spent in the community, he served in various menial roles, mostly in the hospital kitchen, but he became known within and beyond the Carmelites for his quite remarkable and serene faith, and his simple but dynamic experience of "the presence of God." Although he was a comparatively uneducated layman, Brother Lawrence received many letters and other requests from Christians anxious to find similar reality and confidence in their own spiritual lives. Even bishops and other church dignitaries turned to him with problems and doubts about their faith.

To all, Brother Lawrence gave the same answers: stop putting your trust in human rules, devotional exercises, and acts of penance. Instead, exercise a living, obedient faith in God. Live as though he were beside you and with you all the time—*as indeed he is.* Seek to do what he wants, as and when he commands it, and make his command your joy and chief pleasure. The person who lives like that will be fully human, completely Christian, and genuinely happy.

Of course, Brother Lawrence had his critics, both inside and outside the Community. Some felt he was pretending to a knowledge of God not available to ordinary people. Others saw his claims to extraordinary delights and raptures from God's presence as affronts to sober faith and reverence.

But the testimony of those who knew him was that here was a man who walked with God. Brother Lawrence, like few men since Bible times, it would seem, had found—or been shown—the secret of a happy, holy relationship with God. Certainly *The Practice of the Presence of God*—the title given to the collection of his "conversations" and "letters"—has to be included in any list of the really great devotional books of the Christian religion.

However, like many other great but ancient books, it poses enormous problems for the modern reader. The stilted eighteenth-century English of most of the available translations does nothing to make the thoughts of a seventeenth-century Frenchman relevant or dynamic to twentieth-century Christians, and the whole setting of his life and times serves to heighten the sense of remoteness from our present-day tensions and problems.

And yet I believe Brother Lawrence has a message of startling relevance to modern Christians. After all, the modern world makes it harder and harder to live a "spiritual" life. All around us a dehumanizing process is at work: machines replacing hands, computers replacing minds, psychotherapy replacing prayer. And while these things are not bad in themselves, taken together with the accelerating advances of science, the turbulent tempo of life, and the external tensions of events, they have conspired to produce a society that has little time for humanity and even less for God. So how does a twentieth-century Christian set about living the Christian life in this sort of situation? How can we be "spiritual" in a materialistic and mechanistic society?

The traditional answers seem to offer us little practical help. The disciplines of meditation, prayer, study of the Bible, and so on are less and less regarded. The whole concept of silence, for example, is foreign to the age of radio and television.

But Brother Lawrence cuts right through these objections. What he is saying—if only we could see it in *our* setting—is timeless in its relevance. The man who could practice the presence of God in a kitchen has something worthwhile to say to the person who misses the presence of God in the accounting department. If he found a secret of serenity under pressure and tension (and he did), then we, *more* than our Christian predecessors, need to listen to him. He is the man for our times.

This book is, then, an attempt to re-interpret Brother Lawrence for twentieth-century readers. It is not simply a new translation, because if it were, all the problems of background and history would still separate him from us. Instead, I have taken the considerable liberty of transposing the Brother Lawrence of the past into the immediate present—from a monastery kitchen near Paris to a hospital kitchen in modern Boston. All the settings are changed; and the conversations become part of the endless search by contemporary Christians for a faith that is real and existential enough to survive and flourish in the unpromising soil of today.

So I have invented a new environment for "Lawrence Herman," and a new set of friends. But I have taken considerable pains to see that every opinion he expresses—every answer to a question—is substantially authentic "Brother Lawrence." Obviously the illustrations become modern ones (cars, planes, trade fairs), but the ideas are his, and can all be traced back to things he said that are recorded in his "Conversations."

Where the letters are concerned, there was less need to take liberties. Apart from giving his correspondents a modern setting, there was no need to do more than put his own forthright and burning love for God and for them into thoroughly modern language. Soldiers still get injured by activities in active service. Men of sixty-four still worry that they are "finished." People in pain still wonder what possible purpose for God or humankind is achieved by their suffering. To each, Brother Lawrence—alias Laurie, "the happy man"—has words of deep significance to say.

This man gave no glib answers. In that, at least, he seems incredibly "modern." He hated trivial devotion and half-hearted commitment. His letters are shining examples of honesty and integrity—even when he knew his words would hurt before they healed. He was a *great* man, and a great Christian. Without agreeing with every word he uttered, and without starting a new cult, modern Christians can expect to learn things from him that will revolutionize their lives.

Under the Chestnut Tree

The first time I saw Laurie was the third of August 1964, and the last time I saw him was just three weeks ago. This book is all about him—in fact, most of it is by him—but we had to wait until he died before we could put it all together. He hated publicity of any kind, and if he had had his way no one would ever read a word of what he had written, and nothing would ever be reported of the things he said and did.

But some of us—his friends and colleagues at the hospital where he worked, and a few others—felt that people had a right to know about him. We believed that Laurie was different in one vitally important way from anybody we'd ever met. It's hard to pin it down, or describe what he was like, without sounding very "religious" and pious—and Laurie was never like that.

The fact is, he lived his life—an ordinary, hard-working, busy, and sometimes painful life—in God's company. Everyone who met Laurie, whether they were Christians, agnostics, or even atheists, had to admit there was this "difference" about him. It wasn't just that he believed in God, or that he said his prayers, or that he witnessed to Jesus Christ (though he did all three). It was much more than that . . . he was in touch with God. He knew God. He lived in the presence of God every moment of every day. And if that sounds stupid, embarrassing, or strange, then you never knew Laurie.

At any rate, some of us feel that Laurie had discovered something that changed the whole quality of living. The rest of us would worry, and rush around and get ulcers or take tranquilizers—and there he'd be, serene and smiling in the middle of it all, doing twice as much work as we did, without panic or complaint, and finding time to help those who were worried and to spread the inner peace that was his own, personal trade mark. We tried to be Christians. We tried to pray. We tried to relate our faith to the changing, chaotic world around us, to our daily work, and to the problems of suffering, loneliness, and fear. But Laurie seemed to do it without trying.

The Christian life—what the books call "the spiritual life"—seemed almost impossible for us in the modern world. Where could we be quiet? Where could we find tranquility? Where was God to be found in the jungle of machines and the throbbing clamor of the rush hour? Yet Laurie seemed to walk calmly through it all. He was unquestionably "spiritual"—but not because he had copped out of the modern world. He created his own world of peace in the clatter of the hospital kitchen. He fashioned tranquility out of a half-hour lunch break in a locker room. He knew God, and talked with him, and seemed to live his whole day in God's presence.

The result was that those who knew Laurie felt they knew God, too. Nobody else we have ever known had this remarkable effect on people—of drawing them closer to God, whoever they were.

So we decided to produce this memorial volume (again we can imagine what Laurie would have said about *that!*), because we believe that this ordinary man in an ordinary job had a quality of sanity and faith that usually eludes modern man; and that he had found an answer to the sort of problems that worry and distress many good Christians as well. He would never have written a book about it, simply because he never believed what he had discovered was anything but the commonplace level of Christian experience. Probably it *should* be. Anyway, we hope that, just as knowing him and being his friends helped us to share his kind of life with God, so reading what Laurie said and did may help many others to find in all the excitement and confusion of the modern world the quiet inner peace that comes through living in the very presence of a God with whom there is "no variation or shadow due to change."

I first met Laurie when I went down to the Special Diets kitchen to check a delivery note for eggs. I was the food buyer for the hospital, and the S.D. kitchen was my biggest problem, with some patients needing extra protein, fat-free foods, or even particular kinds of fruit that had to be specially ordered through importers. I can't remember what the problem was with the eggs—probably the total on the order didn't tally with the total on the delivery note.

Well, there was this new man in the kitchen—new to me, anyhow. He was short and slightly bald, and wore round, cheap glasses. His white hospital coat was much too long for him, but it was spotlessly clean—a rare sight in our kitchens at that time.

But the first thing you noticed about Laurie was his smile. It wasn't big and hearty, and it wasn't a smirk or a grin. It had the sort of genuineness that makes you realize how seldom you see a real smile. It made you feel welcomed, relaxed, at home. At once you knew you were with someone who had a capacity for enjoyment, an inner contentment, and a love of people. I know that sounds ridiculously exaggerated for an immediate reaction to one smile, but then you never saw the smile!

He introduced himself as Laurie and explained that he'd just been transferred to the S.D. kitchen. We quickly cleared up the egg mystery (whatever it was) and then as it was coffee-break time he poured me a cup and invited me to sit down and drink it with him.

"I think I've seen you at the Christian Fellowship a couple of times, haven't I?" he said.

I'd only been a couple of times and I couldn't remember having seen him there, so I answered lamely, "Yes . . . I go when I can."

"You're a Christian, then?" The smile was hypnotizing me.

"I try to be," I replied.

"I don't," he said. "I gave up trying the day God taught me to trust him."

Now if anyone else had said that to me—the words were so confident, presumptuous, pious—I would have tuned him out right then. But Laurie could say it without offense and make it sound (as indeed it was) like a simple statement of fact. I found myself asking him when this had happened.

"When I was eighteen. It was strange, really. I was out for a walk in the woods near Sudbury trying to think through some problems that had been on my mind for months. I'd been brought up to be a regular church-goer, and for all my conscious life I'd believed in God and wanted to please him. I'd assumed this was done by deliberate acts of worship, by prayer and study, by discipline and self-control—you know the sort of thing. And I was discouraged because, instead of getting better as I got older, I found I was actually getting worse. The harder I tried, the more I failed. I just couldn't see why God, who was supposed to be all-powerful, couldn't do a little miracle and fill me with instant goodness. Little miracle!—God forgive me!

"At any rate, I was walking along, thinking about these things, when I came to a very beautiful chestnut tree just north of the Post Road. I'd been watching it all year—the leaves coming fresh and green from the buds, the flowers opening up in early summer . . . and now it was loaded with chestnuts. The branches were quite weighed down with them.

"I sat under the tree—it's a lovely spot, near the Wayside Inn— and suddenly, like a ray of light bursting in my mind, I got the answer.

"It's hard to explain, but this is how it came to me. In the winter, this old tree was bare, stripped of its leaves, apparently dead. With the spring the new life flowed up from the soil through its trunk and branches, reaching each branch and twig and pushing out the fresh leaves and new growth. Then, later, the flowers and finally the chestnuts appeared, until on this still, sunny September day I could sit in its shade and see the wonderful crop of chestnuts on its branches.

"I was like the tree in winter. Myself, I was nothing—dead, barren, without fruit. And, like the tree, I couldn't change by struggling or sheer effort. I, too, must wait for the hand of my Maker to touch me with life, and change my winter of barren unfruitfulness—in his own time—into first the spring of new life and then the summer and fall of flower and fruit.

"Suddenly I saw what 'providence' is all about—it's simply believing that God has the power and the will to do all things well for us, if we will only submit to his loving, patient rule. And that nothing we can do—beyond trusting him—will speed up his will or make things happen that he isn't ready to do in us.

"At that moment, sitting there on the grass, my acts of worship, my attempts at discipline—all the effort I had put into trying to please God—were swallowed up in an enormous sense of love for him. The One who patiently led the trees and the plants through their seasons would also lead me, if I would only submit to his loving and powerful hand.

"I did. It was a real and true conversion, the result of the overwhelming sight of the majesty and love of God, of his providence and wisdom. I have learned more of his ways since then, and I know him better now and find greater joy in his company than I did on that day years ago. But I honestly cannot say that I love him any more now than at that moment, because there is a limit to the love humans can feel, and I believe at that instant I reached it in my love for a God so good, so patient, and so powerful."

We talked on—I wanted to know more about his conversion—until eleven-fifteen, which was the official, but customarily ignored limit of the coffee break. At that point, Laurie put away the cups and went back to the carrots he had been shredding. As I left, he said he'd enjoyed our conversation and hoped we could talk together again.

All He Really Wants Is Me

"Hi! May I join you?"

I looked up to see Laurie smiling at me, the steam from his soup giving his already cherubic face a quite disturbingly other-worldly glow.

"Why, sure. Sit down."

"I thought the fried fish looked rather good." He began to spread his wares out on the table—soup (tomato), fried fish and chips, sweet roll, butterscotch pudding, and a cup of the cafeteria's own rather strong brew of coffee.

I was about to make my own little joke about deep fried cod, when I checked myself. It wasn't that Laurie didn't enjoy a joke, but I remembered he always muttered a "grace" over his lunch, and somehow it seemed incongruous to ask a man to ridicule a fish for which he had just given thanks to God. You see—he was having an effect on me already.

Somebody had left a copy of the *Globe* on the table, and my eye caught the headline about a mass murder in Los Angeles.

"Grim, isn't it?" I commented, nodding toward the paper. "I just can't understand why people do such horrible things, can you?"

"Oh, yes," he replied, his eyes suddenly catching mine, "I can. Honestly, nothing surprises me about the human race and its evils. It used to, I'll admit. It used to worry me a lot. I would ask myself how men and women made in the image of God could behave like this—and how God could allow it."

He sipped his soup slowly.

"But when I got around to thinking about it seriously, I realized what a mistake I had been making. After all, my conversion had awakened in me a great love for God—you remember, we were talking about it the other day in the kitchen—and the basis of that love was my amazement that someone as pure and holy as he is should offer love, and tenderness, and forgiveness to a person as awkward, disobedient, and failing as I am.

"Well, if I, in the light of all God's love and goodness to me, still find sinful thoughts and reactions a problem, what should I expect of people who have never known him? Quite frankly, far from being surprised at all the misery and evil in the world—things like this murder, here—I'm surprised there isn't more, considering how desperate people must be without God."

I toyed with my Swiss steak and tried to put an elusive anxiety into words.

"Yes, I can see that, Laurie—in a way. I realize that people in rebellion against God are capable of very great evils . . . and I suppose it *is* rather stupid, really, to be surprised when we find people acting in exactly the way the Bible says they will. But—well, isn't there *anything* to be done about it? I mean, do we just wash our hands of it and say, 'There, look what a mess you're in without God. Serves you right!'?"

"No. No, not at all." Laurie spoke firmly. "That would be to imply that God has thrown up his hands and that the world is no longer his."

"Well, what do we do then?"

"For myself," he said, his eyes glued to his food (you couldn't take risks with the cafeteria cod), "I pray for those whose sins become public property—I mean, I *really* pray for them, as needing the love and mercy of God. And then I leave the whole thing to him, believing that God can and will, in his own good time, put right all the wrongs and injustices and sorrows of the world."

"And don't you feel bound to do what you can to put them right?"

"What I can, yes. But I realize that what *I* can do is so very little compared to the great need. That's no reason for not doing it, but it's a very good reason for believing that perfect justice, and perfect mercy, will one day come from God himself, and he will put right what we are helpless to deal with."

Writing down his words now, years after he spoke them, I'm aware of something that I was completely ignorant of at the time— that they could sound smug and unfeeling, as though he were saying, "Don't stew about human suffering and injustice; it'll be all right someday."

All I can say is, that wasn't how it came to me across the small square table. Laurie's eyes were bright, alive with love, not hard with judgment, as he spoke. And when he said he *really* prayed for those whose sin hit the headlines, I knew that meant more than saying words about them: it meant that he would make their burdens his. I suppose you could say Laurie's views were those of a sensitive realist. He knew the heart of humankind, and he knew the heart of God.

Anyway, halfway through the dessert I asked Laurie how things were going in the hospital kitchen. I'd heard that they'd had two kitchen staff off sick and that things had been pretty hectic.

"Fine," he replied, without even stopping to think. "Fine. We're busy, you know . . . but it's a very satisfying job."

I was going to ask about the staff problems, when a shout made me look over toward the counter. I was just in time to see Selinda catch her elbow on a cart and drop a grossly overladen tray of plates, cups, and cutlery. The explosion of metal and china was followed almost instantly by a great burst of laughter and applause. Selinda was very large and very clumsy—qualities that were considered to qualify her to be the butt of most of the hospital wits. In fact, one group of fellows and girls in a corner near the door began a chant of "B-u-t-t-e-r-f-i-n-g-e-r-s."

I turned back to say to Laurie how thoughtless it was of them to tease her. But he had left his seat, and was down on his knees near the counter picking up the broken pieces.

The noise died down, and eventually Laurie came back to finish the remains of his meal.

"Poor Selinda," he said, though his eyes were smiling. "They say lazy people take the most pains. Funny,"—a reminiscent chuckle—"that was a lesson I learned the hard way, too."

I looked interested, guessing some story from his past was coming up. It was.

"I used to work for a big banker—a Canadian, he was, head of their Boston office. He had a lovely Colonial home in Lexington . . . this was a while after my 'conversion,' remember? Well, my job was really to be a sort of assistant cook. I stood in for the chef on his days off, and the rest of the time I helped prepare vegetables, clean the kitchen, and give a hand with general housework and odd jobs.

"The truth is I'm not all that good with my hands, especially when I'm nervous . . . which I often was in those days. And also I always wanted to get things done as quickly as possible.

"The result was that I soon had a reputation as a butterfingers. Too many cups in the sink, too many plates on a tray, and even—one horrible afternoon—too many antique vases on the table I was supposed to be polishing. I was told the vase had cost over five hundred dollars . . . when it was all in one piece, you understand.

"The incredible thing was how kind everybody was about it. I found this more worrying than the actual breakages. No matter what I did my employer was always gentle and understanding, and so was the chef, for that matter. It began to upset me—that I should go unpunished when I was such a destructive menace around the house.

"In the end I couldn't stand it any longer—aren't we strange creatures? I believe I'd have stuck it out if they'd asked me to pay for the breakages out of my wages! But I decided I'd leave and go somewhere where my criminal carelessness would get its just rewards. For some obscure reason I felt both God and I would be satisfied if only I were made to suffer for my faults. So—believe it or not—I came here. I'd heard the work was hard, and the Food Service manager a real, old-fashioned disciplinarian.

"But what happened? Certainly nothing like I'd expected. From the day I arrived I've enjoyed every minute of it. Far from being a sort of punishment for my failures, every day I've spent here has been tremendously satisfying. No one has punished me, but God has given me a completely new understanding of himself.

"I suppose the whole thing is a picture of our inability to grasp what 'grace' really means—the completely undeserved favor of God. Like me in the banker's house, we find it harder to accept grace, tenderness, and forgiveness than we do to accept punishment and pain. We want to *earn* God's approval . . . but even the best we can do would fall far short of that. God *gives* it to us, in the middle of our failures—if we put our trust in him, and love him, and give him first place.

"And that's the key. I used to spend a lot of time thinking up ways to please God—new acts of devotion, petty sacrifices of frivolities, longer periods of prayer and fasting. But now I've learned that all he really wants is *me*, and that these very 'things' that were meant to please him could be distractions from living all the time as though he were here.

"And he is. He's really here . . . not just 'in heaven,' but right here in the cafeteria and down below in the Special Diets kitchen. If I've got him, what else could I possibly need?"

He glanced at his watch.

"Which reminds me," he said, grinning, "that when I get on my hobby horse, I sometimes forget about the work I'm paid to do! I've *got* to go."

"Look," I said, "Laurie . . . I want to know more—about living near God, and all that."

"Fine," he said, stacking his plates carefully. "If that's what you really want, come see me again—some lunchtime? Or evening?"

The Joys of the Road

"Hello, Laurie. Welcome back."

He looked up, and the eyes lit up. Nice—how he always seemed genuinely glad to see you.

"Hi! Yes . . . and boy, am I glad to be back."

I couldn't resist a laugh.

"Give *me* four days in Miami Beach in exchange for this place, and I wouldn't be glad to be back."

Laurie shook his head.

"I'm just not cut out for that sort of thing. Frankly, I wasn't looking forward to it."

"Tell me about it," I said, sitting down and nodding toward the electric clock over the kitchen door, which showed coffee time. He took the hint and put on the pot.

"Well, Ramsden was going, of course. It was an international display put on by manufacturers of diet foods—a sort of small-scale trade fair, I suppose. There's a lot of new stuff coming on the market—most of it for slimming, so far as I can see, but special protein foods and vitamin products—you can imagine the sort of thing.

"Well, as I say, Ramsden was going, but something came up and he asked me to go instead—keep my eyes open and bring home samples of stuff we might find useful. There were films and demonstrations, too—people were there from all over the nation, and Europe, too.

"It was all a bit over my head. I'm not a qualified dietitian. I'm a cook, let's face it. I've picked up a good deal, but I'm not a businessman and I'm not an expert in anything. Still, as Ramsden couldn't go and somebody—apparently—had to represent the hospital, I couldn't refuse."

"But it went off all right?"

Again, the laugh.

"You *could* say so! The flight was pretty bad. You know I've got this weak ankle—well, it 'went' just as we were boarding, and every time the plane ran into turbulence it was agony. Still, it wasn't for long—and it stopped as soon as we landed.

"The display was fascinating and people were most helpful. I found that I was meeting the right people, without organizing it, and Ramsden was wild about the stuff I brought back."

"So you were worrying about nothing?"

"In a way. The truth is, I'd somehow managed to forget that going to a convention in Florida could be God's business just as much as working here in the kitchen—or leading a Bible study. I'd allowed the fact that it was an unwelcome job to blind me to the fact that God was calling me to do it.

"Anyway, a few days before I left I saw what was happening. I said to God, 'Lord, it's your work I'm doing, here in Boston, or down in Florida. I can't do even my daily work properly without your help, let alone these special jobs. Take away my uneasiness and give me a calm and trusting attitude, and help me to do my work to your glory here, there, or anywhere.'"

"And he did?"

Laurie looked surprised at my question. "Of course. Have you ever known him to fail?"

The coffee was poured by now, and we still had ten minutes of our coffee break left. I mentioned something that Laurie had just touched on, and that had been on my mind for weeks.

"Laurie, your saying that makes me think of something else. Prayer."

His pale eyes crinkled at the corners, as though inviting me to proceed.

"You seem to find prayer so easy, Laurie—just like talking to"—I was going to say "someone you know," and realized that was exactly what it was, in his case—"talking to another human being. And God talks back to you. I don't find it easy at all . . . in fact, I have to *make* myself pray. How did you get into the way of turning so simply to God in prayer?"

"Human being!" Laurie smiled and repeated the phrase. "Another human being. Now if you'd said person, I'd have said that was the heart of it.

"God *is* a person. He's a personal God, not just a great creative Force. How else should we talk to him but as a person?

"Still, you asked how I got into the habit of talking to him so simply, and that's a fair question. It wasn't always so simple, by any means.

"From the time when God became real to me, I knew that communicating with him—two-way communication—was the most important thing in the world. To communicate with everyone else and be deaf and dumb to God is to turn our priorities upside down, isn't it?

"Naturally, I don't mean communicating with him on a basis of equality, but on a basis of dependence. I had to talk with him, and he with me, because only he perfectly knows my condition and circumstances and only he can perfectly guide me through life. I knew that I must learn to refer everything I did to him . . . everything. That seems to me just plain common sense. An airline pilot keeps in constant touch with ground control because they know things he doesn't and can't know. And that is why I keep in touch with God."

I said that I could see that, but though I knew it was important, I still found it difficult.

"At first I found it difficult, too. To say it's important to talk with God and refer everything to him isn't quite the same thing as saying it's easy. To begin with, it requires discipline and persistent effort. And I mean that.

"Don't be fooled. Because I can talk with God so easily and simply today doesn't mean that it was always so. The price you have to pay is willingness—willingness to control your mind and thoughts, willingness to submit to God's discipline, willingness to keep at it even when you seem to make little progress. Nothing worth having is easily achieved. Acts of the will are the ones that matter most.

"But after a while—and I don't mean years and years, but months and even weeks, if you really mean business you will find that what was hard effort has become a great joy. Because you love God, and know he loves you, the strain quickly goes out of the relationship, and his love excites you—that's the only word that really describes it—*excites* you with a longing to be with him and talk with him.

"You've seen people learning to drive a car? At first they have to concentrate on the techniques—you see their faces tight with concentration as they try to find the right gear, and so on. But as they master the technical side, and get plenty of practice, they stop 'driving' and start 'traveling'—until the time comes when driving is quite automatic and even subconscious, and they begin to appreciate the 'joys of the road.' "

It was my turn to laugh, because Laurie wasn't a driver. But I got the point, and it was a good one.

"O.K. I can see that, Laurie. But how do you go about the 'techniques' of praying? Do you have set hours of prayer . . . what does Foster call it? A 'quiet time'?"

"Well—yes, I do have set times of prayer, and I believe they are a useful discipline, especially for a beginner . . . a learner, as you might say. But personally I don't worry much about them, and it wouldn't bother me if I were kept from keeping them at all. Put it this way: I don't *need* them. God is no nearer to me during my 'quiet time' than he is at this very moment in the kitchen; and prayer is no more real when it is said formally, on my knees by my bed, than when I say it informally over the sink or the oven. I really can't wait until ten at night or seven in the morning to refer some vital matter to God. I need him too much and too often to be able to leave things until a particular hour of the day. And his presence is so real that there is no danger that I'll forget to talk with him if I don't make an appointment with him!"

"So you do recommend me to have set times of prayer?"

"Yes—definitely. But not as an end in themselves, so that you say to yourself as you get off your knees in the morning, 'Well, that's my praying done for today.' That's just a bit of it—a concentrated dose, if you like. Set times of prayer are valuable in order to form a habit of conversation with God, and—as I said—referring all we do to him. They aren't the end itself, but means to an end. The end is God: being with him, living in his presence and under his control. You can't do that if you try to ration contact with God to twenty minutes twice a day or whatever it is."

Time was up. Laurie glanced at the clock.

"Look," he said, "We're just getting on to something very important. Why not come around to my room tonight and we'll pick up where we've stopped now?"

Problems with Prayer

I didn't know the street existed, and it took me longer than I had expected to track it down, even though it wasn't more than half a mile from the hospital. Laurie had said "Come about eight" but it was a good deal later when I stood on the imposing front steps of a big old brownstone tenement and looked for the bell. I had always assumed he lived at the hospital.

The door was a double one, with dark glass windows, and everything seemed to be painted a dingy dark brown. Then I saw a small brass plate and by it an enormous, antique doorbell. The plate said "Brotherhood of St. Vincent," which startled me but I pushed the bell and waited. All seemed dark and silent inside.

After some minutes a light came on somewhere along the entrance hall, and to my relief Laurie opened the door.

"I'm a bit late, I'm afraid . . ." I began.

"Oh, forget it! Everybody has a job finding us the first time."

I went into the hall and he led the way up a wide flight of stone stairs.

"Who's the 'us'?" I asked. "The Brothers of St. Vincent?"

"Yes. It's just a small Order—lay brothers, doing what the Rule calls 'practical works of mercy.' Vincent was a deacon, you see—ours is a serving Order."

He stopped at a plain door, painted the inevitable church hall brown again, and showed me into his room. It was small and very plainly furnished—an iron bed, a small table, two chairs, and an old-fashioned iron radiator . . . and a simple wooden cross on the wall above the fireplace.

"I didn't know you were a . . ."

"A monk?" he prompted, smiling. "I'm not. I'm just a lay Christian, like you, except that I've submitted myself to the Rule of this small Brotherhood. I do my ordinary day's work at the hospital, and live in the community here. There's nothing mystical or odd about it, I assure you."

He nodded toward one of the two chairs, and I sat on it.

"I'll get a kettle on," he said. "We have a gas burner out in the corridor—primitive, but effective."

He left me alone for a minute or two while he saw to this, and I tried to adjust myself to this other picture of Laurie. It was all a bit . . . well, ecclesiastical. I'd never thought of him as anything quite so *churchy*.

Tea poured out, Laurie raised the subject we'd agreed to discuss—my problems with prayer. He suggested I start off by raising the difficulties I experienced—because, as he put it, "problems are very personal things, and so is prayer."

"Well," I said, "probably the worst thing of all is what one friend of mine used to call 'dry spells'—every now and again I hit a bad patch . . . it may last a month, or even longer . . . when I just can't get any *joy* out of praying. I feel as though it's just a routine, and my words aren't getting beyond the ceiling. Usually, I admit, I give up and don't pray at all until something or other starts me off again."

Laurie nodded. "Yes, I know the experience exactly."

"You mean—you've had it?"

He smiled. "Of course. I don't suppose a Christian exists who hasn't gone through what you've just described.

"Funny enough, I think part of the answer is connected with the sort of thing that belonging to this Order involves. As I told you the other day, in general I don't rely too much on set times and patterns of prayer—I feel as near God . . . nearer, perhaps . . . in the hospital kitchen as in the chapel here, or kneeling by my bed. I think I said that when we first adopt the practice of prayer, set times are important to help us submit ourselves to God, but then they become less necessary as we learn to be with God and talk with him all the time—actually, they can even become distractions, at times.

"Much the same thing applies to the times of 'dryness.' For me, that's when the Rule becomes not a distraction, but a prop for my faith—or lack of it. I believe God sends these 'dry spells'—I like your friend's phrase—to test our love for him. Does 'absence make the heart grow fonder'? Or is it a case of 'out of sight, out of mind'? If we can only love God when we feel he is near us, then our love is immature and feeble. So God withdraws himself, sometimes, to test our love. And that is when our inner discipline—and these 'outer' disciplines of set times and patterns—should take over. Fidelity . . . faithfulness . . . is then the chief virtue."

"But it's hard, isn't it, Laurie? I mean, when the very act of being faithful seems irritating or unreal."

"Hard? Sure it is. There's an emotional, 'feeling' element in prayer and when that disappears, as it does in these dry times, then what was formerly a pleasure can be dull and may even feel 'unreal.' But love isn't *just* emotion. I mean, it's a relationship, isn't it? And whether I 'feel' it or not, I know God loves me and I know his will is best."

"O.K. I can see that keeping at it faithfully, even when God seems distant, is part of the answer. Do you just wait, then, for God to 'come back,' as it were?"

Laurie smiled. "He isn't far from any of us . . . ever. But I see what you mean." He put down his empty cup, and thought for a moment. "Would you know what I meant if I said, 'Make an act of resignation'?"

I shook my head.

"Well, it's jargon, I suppose. By an 'act of resignation' I mean a conscious and deliberate submission to the will of God."

"Say that again?"

"A point where you say to God, 'Lord, you are my God. You know what is best for me. You only can give me true joy. All my life lies in your hands. If this present dryness is because of my rebellion or willfulness, or lack of faith, I here and now submit myself again totally to you, without any reserve, not claiming your presence as a right, but resigning myself completely to your good and perfect will.' I have found—and so have others—that one such 'act of resignation,' sincerely made, often not only ends the drought, but leads into new experiences of God."

I nodded, there not being much else to say, and raised another thing that had been bothering me.

"Right. But how do I make sure that I don't just simply 'forget' God? I must admit sometimes, at the end of a hectic day, perhaps, I've found myself in bed and suddenly realized I'd clean forgotten about praying. And often I go hours on end—days, I suppose, sometimes—without ever giving him a thought at all. That's terrible, isn't it?"

"I shall probably shock you," Laurie said, "but, honestly, no . . . it isn't terrible. Fortunately, God knows us better than we know ourselves. 'He remembers that we are only dust.' There's no point in getting all uptight about 'not thinking' of him. He's still there, whether I think about him or not. He doesn't change.

"When I find I haven't thought of God for a good while, I don't get depressed and guilty about it, but simply admit to him that I'm pretty forgetful (which I am), and then remind myself of his faithfulness and love.

"You may find this surprising—I mean, now that you know I'm part of this 'Order'—but I set very little importance indeed on all these penances and painful exercises that some people use to overcome their guilt at spiritual failures. Indeed"—he leaned forward, as though sharing something very significant—"I feel many sincere Christians don't get anywhere in the Christian life because they stick at penances and so-called 'exercises' instead of pressing on past them to the object of the whole thing, which is love of God. In the end, it makes them dry and self-centered, trying to fight their way back to God when he's right beside them all the time, waiting for them to turn to him and trust him. Faith . . . that's the key. Faith is the beginning and end of it all."

"I haven't got much faith," I said—and it came out more truly than I had intended.

Laurie lifted an eyebrow. "It's not a commodity, you know. Like coffee or toothpastes. It's more like a plant. It grows."

"I'm sure it grows for you, Laurie," I said. "But for me—well, I believe in God, and that's about it."

"Actually, that *is* it," Laurie cut in. "That's exactly it.

"When I first joined the Order—soon after my conversion—I found I was expected to spend several hours a day in prayer. The Prior gave me lots of advice and several little books of meditation, but I'm afraid I ignored the advice and left the books on my shelf. You see, that day in the woods I had met God . . . a God who was really there. I didn't see how exercises and forms could bring him any closer than he had been that day without them.

"So, I spent the hours appointed for private prayer in thinking of God."

It was my turn to lift an eyebrow, and Laurie noticed and smiled.

"All right, I know that sounds vague. But I didn't just kneel there and list his attributes, or recite acts of devotion to him. I set out first to think through his divine existence—that he really and truly and objectively *exists*, as Someone quite other and apart from me, his creature. That was first, and I thought of him and all I knew of him from the Scriptures and in my experience until I was totally convinced that *God is*. I had no intention of spending my life in the presence of a Being who was simply a figment of my imagination.

"Then I spent hours letting that tremendous truth impress itself deeply on my heart—my feelings, if you like. Slowly, by letting my mind lead my heart, and by letting the light of faith shine into my feelings, I came to a point where my faith was alive and growing. I had absorbed, first, the knowledge, and then the love of God, and I resolved to do all I could to live from then on in a continual sense of his presence and, if possible, never to forget him again. There was no studied reasoning to prove the existence of God, and no elaborate meditation to inflame my devotion to him. But I had been in his presence—the living God—and I never wished to leave it ever again."

The Purpose of Suffering

Robert looked as surprised as I had the first time I climbed the stairs to Laurie's room. Every footstep squeaked alarmingly and echoed between the bare stone walls and the unrelieved expanses of brown paint.

"Well, you told me it would be a shock, but I didn't quite associate old Laurie with this sort of place."

I laughed, and led the way on to a small landing. Laurie must have heard us coming, for the door opened before I could knock, and the darkness suddenly was split with light from his room. Robert followed me in, his eyes taking in the simple furnishings and religious objects, and then Laurie was fussing around making coffee and soon we were both oblivious to the surroundings. When we were all comfortably sipping our hot coffee, Laurie raised again the subject we'd asked him about in the canteen that very day.

"Now, let's see, we were talking about Marion, weren't we? What was it that was bothering you, Robert—I mean, beyond the thing we were all saddened about, that she was so ill and not likely to get well again?"

"It was this matter of—what did you call it, John?—'pointless suffering.' Marion's just one example, but it's happening all the time. It's . . . it's as if a malignant enemy were following us, waiting to pounce out of the shadows and ruin our lives. Surely that can't be God's will?"

Laurie thought for a moment, gazing at his steaming cup in silence.

"Why do you say 'pointless,' Robert? How do you know Marion's suffering is 'pointless'?"

"Well, it's hard to see . . ."

"Of course it's hard to see. We've got such a limited perspective—a sort of 'worm's eye view' of life. It might look quite different from God's viewpoint. It might even look quite different from Marion's, especially when it's all over."

"That's fair enough, Laurie," I chipped in. "But surely that's rather cold comfort to Marion? I mean—as she actually goes through all the searing pain . . . it must be hard to keep telling yourself, 'There's some point in this, somewhere.'"

Robert leaned forward, and tossed in the question we'd both been avoiding—not just that night, but every time we'd talked with Laurie on the subject of pain.

"Look, Laurie," he said, "Forgive me for putting it like this, but there's no point in beating about the bush. You're very stoical and fatalistic about suffering, in theory. But how would you react if it were happening to you?"

"Not fatalistic." Laurie got that in quickly. "That's pagan. Not even stoical, really, because I'm not at all brave or courageous. More—how can I put it?—*trusting* . . . trusting that my all-knowing God knows best.

"To be frank, I *do* expect that one day, perhaps quite soon, I shall experience some great pain of body or mind. As a matter of fact, my health has never been all that great, and at my age I must be prepared for some illness and pain.

"But the way I look at it is this: I ask myself what could be the worst thing that could possibly happen to me. The answer is crystal clear—it would be to lose this sense of God's presence, which I have enjoyed for many years. That would be the ultimate disaster and the bitterest pain—and my mind recoils in horror from the thought of it. But God has assured me, in his own written promises, and in the assurance he has given me in my own heart, that he will 'never leave me nor forsake me.'

"That means that, whatever else, the worst imaginable thing *simply cannot ever happen to me,* and compared with that no pain of body or mind has any real power over me. After all, the greatest pains—or the greatest pleasures—of this world can't be compared with what I have already experienced of both kinds in the spiritual state. Once I am sure that God will deliver me from all spiritual evils, through the blood of Jesus Christ, I find that physical evils are rather cut down to size—seen in their true perspective."

"Do you mean," I asked, "that you would simply grin and bear them?"

Laurie permitted himself one of his wonderful, understanding smiles.

"No, of course not. What I mean is that if God has perfectly provided for the greater evil—spiritual pain and loss—I am completely confident that he can and will take care of the lesser evil of physical pain. I believe that he would give me strength to bear whatever evil he permitted to happen to me, and so I don't need to worry about that."

"But that still doesn't answer the charge that such suffering is pointless." Robert was sticking to his case.

"Well—nothing is pointless for the Christian, is it? But sometimes we have to search pretty hard to find what its point is.

"Look—when we set out on the Christian life, our two basic needs are to know Christ and to know ourselves. The interesting thing is, that as we get to know him better, we get to know ourselves better, too—and we find how unworthy we are of the name of 'Christian.' Like the apostle Paul, we judge ourselves 'the foremost of sinners.' We come to see that our fallen natures, so easily drawn to every kind of sin, are responsible for most of the troubles and sorrows of life, both in us and in our circumstances. And we have to admit that whatever pain comes to us is less than we deserve, and to submit ourselves to it, and bear it as long as God calls us to do so, will bring its own spiritual advantages and blessings . . . now, or later. Perfect resignation to God's will—that is, trusting acceptance of it—is the sure way to heaven, and light from heaven floods the path.

"I'm sorry," he added, the smile breaking through again. "That sounded like a sermon."

"And rather a negative one, at that," said Robert (but he was smiling, too). "I can see that there may well be blessing in this kind of fortitude and—what did you call it?—trusting acceptance. But aren't there more positive elements in the Christian life?"

"Yes," I said, before Laurie could reply, "I've often wanted to ask you that. What do we *do*—I mean, actively—to become better Christians . . . What are the basic requirements?"

"You're asking for another sermon!"

"No, just your own experience, Laurie . . . It's a question we often raise at our fellowship meetings, but everybody gives different answers."

"Well, St. Paul said that there are three things that last forever: faith, hope, and love. My experience is that those three are the permanent elements of any person's relationship with God."

"Uh, could you repeat that?" Robert had obviously got lost somewhere in that last sentence.

"Faith, hope, and love are what it's all about," Laurie paraphrased. "Through faith we believe his promises and have hope. Through faith and hope we come to love him, and for love of him we want to please him in everything we do. So faith, hope, and love combined unite us to the will of God. We believe in him, and so we go where he leads. He is our only hope, and so we cling to him whatever comes. And we love him, and so set out to please him by what we think, what we say, what we do.

"Somebody has put it this way: All things are possible to him who believes; they are less difficult to him who hopes; they are not difficult at all to him who loves; and they are easy to him who keeps on doing all three."

Robert was shaking his head.

"It all sounds so impressive," he said, staring at his toes. "And I'm sure you're right. Sitting here I can believe it all, and I honestly think that if I were in a different sort of job—living in a community like this, perhaps, or farming peacefully somewhere, or working as a missionary—I could succeed as a Christian. But how can you think in terms of faith, hope, and love when you spend your working life ankle deep in electronic equipment, always ten minutes behind schedule, and besieged by people who want their machines back yesterday. I can hardly get around to thinking of lunch, let alone thinking of God—and everything I do is so totally *secular*."

Laurie laughed.

"Sounds just like the S.D. kitchen to me. But what makes you think that God is absent from the maintenance shop, but present in the chapel? Where's your doctrine of God? In any case, holiness doesn't depend on changing our jobs, *but in doing for God's sake what we have been used to doing for our own.*

"Seriously—repair the equipment for God, answer the abusive phone calls for God, concentrate fully on the job you're doing for God. He isn't obsessed with *religion*—he's the God of the whole of life. But we need to give it to him, consciously turning it over into his hands. Then whatever we're doing—provided it is not against his will—becomes an act of Christian service.

"In fact, I'd go so far as to say that the very best way of coming closer to God that I have yet discovered—far better than those dreary mechanical 'devotions' recommended by some of the textbooks—is to do my ordinary, everyday business without any view of pleasing people, but as far as I can, purely for the love of God. That was what St. Paul was talking about . . . let me see, where is it?"—he laboriously extracted his Bible from the plain bookcase near his bed—"In Galatians, I think. Yes, here it is: 'Am I now seeking the favor of men, or of God? Or am I trying to please men? If I were still pleasing men, I should not be a servant of Christ.' "

We sat for a moment silent, because there didn't seem to be much more to say. That left Laurie with the last word.

"Honestly, I feel closer to God in the kitchen than I usually do during a chapel service."

All for the All

Dear Fiona,

To be honest, I find your request a very difficult one. On one hand, I long to see you grow in the Christian life, having had a small part in planting the seed of faith in your heart. On the other hand, the experience God has given me is so precious, and so private, that I have always been reluctant to speak of it, or let it be known how he has come to me. Spiritual pride is an ugly and dangerous thing, and too often I feel it at my shoulder.

But how can I refuse you? It is natural, and right, that you should want to feel God's continuing presence. It is part of your birthright as a child of God. And I know you are sincere in this, if only from the number of letters you have written and your determination to wring from me somehow the method (as you call it) by which I found this great blessing from God.

So I am going to tell you—but on one condition. You must not show this letter to anybody else. If I thought for one moment that you would let it be seen, all my longing for your growth in Christ could not persuade me to put these words on paper. However, assuming—as I must—that you will respect my confidence, here is my story.

After my conversion (which you know about) many people pressed various spiritual books and manuals on me, all offering differing, and sometimes conflicting, advice about the Christian life, personal devotions, prayer, and so on. Faced with all these different ways of going to God, I decided to wash my hands of them all. They only served (it seemed to me) to confuse what must surely be an essentially simple thing. All I wanted to know was: how could I put myself completely in God's hands?

This led me to a phrase that kept coming back into my mind: *to give all for the All.* As a concept it seemed so much more clear-cut than the exhortations in the textbooks. He would give—indeed, *has already given*—all, and it is blasphemy to offer less than all to him. There and then I laid myself before God, and renounced, for love of him, everything that was not of God, and began from that moment to live as if there were no one in the world but he and I.

Sometimes I saw myself, where God was concerned, as a criminal in court, looking up at the judge. At other times I saw myself as his favored son, looking up into the eyes of my loving Father. As often as I could I expressed my thanks and worship to him, and I consciously kept my mind in his presence, and called it back whenever it wandered off after other things.

This wasn't easy, of course, but I kept at it. Let me make one thing clear—my attitude was not a product of abject fear, nor of rigid discipline. It was the product of love. When my mind wandered, or got distracted with "worldly" things, I didn't go in for an orgy of remorse, but quietly turned my thoughts back to him. And I practiced this all the time—thinking of God, reminding myself of his goodness, love, and holiness, even in the middle of preparing a high-protein breakfast or dealing with complaints from patients. It's not as difficult as it sounds, once you get away from the idea that there are set times to pray and set times *not* to pray!

Well, that's the way it's been all these years. And imperfect though it has been, the most tremendous blessings have flowed into my life from it. I well realize—I emphasize it to you, Fiona—that these blessings are simply, solely, and entirely of the mercy and goodness of God. No "method" or "technique"—whether mine, or those in the books I mention—can *do* any of it without him. And no one can *be* anything without him—I less than any.

But my experience is that when we are faithful to keep ourselves in his presence, and keep him constantly "before our eyes," it keeps us from willfully offending him, and so preventing his grace and power from flowing into our lives.

But more than that: to live with God always beside us creates in our hearts a holy freedom and—if I may put it in such words—more familiarity with God than all the devotional aids on earth. We are not meant to be cramped, tongue-tied, fearful, or hesitant in his presence. The Son has come to "set us free." What happens, I believe, is that by continually remembering him our sense of the presence of God becomes at first *habitual*, and then delightfully *natural*. That is my "method," if one may use such a word about a practice that is now as normal to me as breathing.

Please don't write to thank me for this letter. Give God thanks, if you wish, for his great goodness to me, which I can never deserve.

May you, and I, and all things praise *him*.

Yours in the Lord,
Laurie

The Touches of God

My dear Bishop,

Forgive me for bothering you with this letter, but you've always helped me so much in the past that I felt you were the right person to turn to for advice, or your opinion, on a subject that disturbs me a good deal.

You know, from some of our past conversations, of the way in which God has blessed me for many years. You were kind enough to say once that if all your clergy and workers enjoyed a similar walk with God most of our problems in Christ would disappear overnight. But you also know of the opinions of some of those I love and respect most, including some in the Brotherhood, who feel otherwise about God's dealings with me, and it is on this that I should be glad to have your thoughts. I have searched through books for the story of a similar experience to mine—to prove that it is not so extreme or peculiar—but have failed to find anything quite like it.

A few days ago a deeply spiritual person took me to one side and told me that the Christian life was a life of grace that began with abject fear of God, grew with the hope of eternal life, and was perfected in a pure love for him—and that we all must go through these three stages.

Now, sir, this is my dilemma: If what he said is true, and exclusively so, then my belief is not true Christian faith at all, and my daily experiences of God are not real, but fantasies. But I *know* it is authentic and that they are genuine touches of God on my life.

For me, these stages of fear, hope, and love have little positive meaning. In fact, they are actually discouraging. That is why, from the day I joined the Brotherhood, I have set myself simply and solely to know and love God *himself*, and to renounce all substitutes and formulas—even religious ones.

I must admit that for about ten years after that, I suffered a great deal, spiritually. Having resolved, like many Christians before me, to meditate frequently on death, judgment, heaven, hell, and similar serious themes, I found that it was my sins that were also in front of my eyes, and my great failure. At times it seemed that events, reason, and even God himself, were against me, and only *faith* stood on my side. But the effect of this was to make me cling to God, at the thought of the great and undeserved kindness he had shown one as sinful and full of failure as I was. And from that came what I can only call a tremendous *appreciation* for God (respect is too weak, reverence too cold—there really isn't a word for it), which itself produced from time to time a sense of great delight and consolation in him.

At that point I was sometimes troubled, I must admit, by the thought that to believe I had received such favors was a colossal presumption—pretending to be at one leap where other and better people only arrived after a lifetime of difficulty. I sometimes even wondered whether it was not a willful delusion, a trick of Satan, and that in truth I was lost.

But eventually, as you know, after some ten years of this tension between great joy and great anxiety, God gave me a profound inward peace, as though my soul had finally arrived at her center and place of rest. I did not *believe* any more than before, but the sense of unrest and conflict was taken away and—thank God—has never returned. And from that day I have tried to walk before God very simply, in faith, in humility, and in love for him, trusting that when I have done what I can, he will do with me what he pleases. I would not take up a piece of paper from the floor against his orders, nor from any motive but from my love of him.

I have, as you know, given up all set forms of devotion and prayers (except those that the rule of Order obliges me to fulfill). I just always enjoy an habitual silent and secret conversation of the spirit with God—and sometimes, I am afraid, this inward joy or rapture is so intense that I have to control myself strongly to keep from disturbing or embarrassing people around me.

Why I am writing to you, sir, is this. Some good men, as I have said, now tell me that I have got it all wrong. They say that it is a delusion, that it is pietistic, too "otherworldly," too remote from the world and its problems, too self-centered.

And I cannot bear that this inexpressible joy, this union with God, should be called delusion. I want nothing but God. If this is delusion on my part, surely God would show me, and put it right? He would not leave me for so long in self-deception. Let him do as he wishes with me. Is that "otherworldly"? I want only him. Is that to be "self-centered"?

But I do not want to defend my own experience of God. Indeed, I do not need to, for he is judge. But, as I have always respected your opinion, and as some of my Christian friends are clearly worried about me, I should be grateful if you would tell me whether what God has done with me is so very exceptional, or so remarkably extreme. Or is it, as I suspect, so very normal that people are afraid of it, and miss, through fear, the love that casts it out?

Yours very sincerely in the Lord,
Laurie

He's Near, and You'll Know It

Sgt. J.F. Conway
FR 228624131
Signal Corps Det 63
A.P.O. New York 09324

Dear John,

How good to hear from you! Naturally we had been wondering how you were getting on—we had heard a little news from Ralph, and we pray for you from time to time at our Fellowship meetings, but it was a great joy for me to hear from you directly, and to find that your main concern now, as it was when you were with us at the hospital, is to know and love and serve God better.

Now—about the matter you raised.

First of all, let me say I wasn't surprised to hear that you had run into difficulties. I must admit I had always expected that someday God would put you to the test in this sort of way. After all, you had things rather easy, hadn't you? A person like you—full of personality, popular, active, and energetic—is always tempted to feel that he can manage life perfectly well on his own, or with just a little help from God. You won't think that again, will you?

About your circumstances. I can, of course, give little advice. You were so eager to join the Army (and I'm not blaming you for that, or saying that it was a wrong decision)—and to see the world. I realize that a small military base in a hostile sheikdom, with nothing but burning sand in every direction, no proper leave for six months, and very little relief from the incessant heat, is not exactly what you expected: but it's what you've got, and whatever you've got has come by God's permission, and is at this moment his will for you. Believe that!

But I gather from your letter that it's not simply the circumstances that have got you down. You rightly see that the true issue is within yourself, and I must say I am glad—yes, *glad*—that this is so. You say God doesn't "come to you" anymore. He will, in his own good time, and when you least expect it. More to the point is, do you "come to God"? From your letter, I believe that you do, and this is why I am glad about what is happening to you. You have not let your depression bury your concern for God. Probably for the first time in your life, you are facing really man-sized difficulties—but that is bringing to the surface a man-sized faith. And that's cause for rejoicing!

So, John—hope in God more than ever. Thank him—as I do now—for the favors he is doing you, especially for the patience and determination he has given you during this difficult and testing time. That in itself is the best possible proof of the care he takes of you. Let that encourage you, and be sure to thank him for it.

I can see how Michael's accident has depressed you. It must have been wonderful to meet him out there after all that time—and what a strange meeting place! I read about the incident, of course, in the papers, but had no idea another former member of our Fellowship was one of those injured by the mine.

As you say, the injury itself (thank God) was not too serious. More serious is the way it has affected both Michael's faith, and yours.

I have always felt—and have told him to his face, in the past— that Michael should really put his mind to growing up as a Christian. His heart is in the right place, his character is excellent, but sometimes he seems to be rather immature in his attitude to things, and a little caught up in "the world." I know it's hard for healthy, lively young men like you two to apply your minds to subjects like death, judgment, and heaven—but there is no way to Christian maturity without it, believe me.

So even this accident, you see, can have a good result, because it can compel you both to turn your minds to serious and important matters. Michael, certainly, will have plenty of time in the hospital to do some real thinking—do urge him, won't you, to see how what has happened to him underlines his need of God? He may feel it proves God has deserted him. But that kind of thinking makes God little more than a good luck mascot. In fact, an accident like this should drive a spiritual man to renew his total trust in God, who goes with him everywhere, and keeps him in joy and pain, in pleasure and sorrow, in life *and in death.*

Turn it all to prayer and faith. That's my advice in a nutshell. Think of God as often as you can, and especially in times of danger. Just a little lifting up of the heart is enough—a little remembrance of God, a brief act of inward worship—even out on patrol, or on guard with a rifle in your hands: God hears and understands. He is near, and you will know it.

Don't think this in any way lessens your ability or efficiency as a soldier. Far from it. The man whose courage is built only on his own resources can never match the man who is drawing on the courage of Christ.

So here is my advice to you both. Think of God as often as you can. Cultivate the habit, by degrees, of turning consciously to him at every opportunity, no matter how briefly. Make these small, holy acts of worship and prayer. No one need see or know (none of those barrack-room bedside dramatics—prayer is not for public performance), and what I am suggesting is not very difficult. All it requires is the will to do it. And it seems to me absolutely necessary for people in your position, whose lives and whose spiritual standing are under constant attack, to know where to turn for help at any moment.

God bless you both. You know I am praying for you, and I trust you pray for all your former colleagues and brothers in Christ here, and for me.

> Yours,
> Laurie

A Low Place for
Grace to Flow

Dear Richard,

Yes, you are right. There *is* a brother in our Society who has had—
and, in fact, daily enjoys—just the experience you describe. I do
know him, and am delighted to tell you a bit about him. Then
perhaps, if you are still interested, you may care to meet him and
decide whether what I am about to tell you is truth or exaggeration.
Anyway, I'm grateful for the opportunity to write to you about him,
because I believe simply recounting what God has done in him and
with him will be a blessing to both of us: me in the telling, and you
in the reading.

The man you describe has been seeking a deeper knowledge of
God for more than forty years. I don't think it would be an over-
statement to say that throughout that time—since his conversion as
a young man—his chief ambition has been to think, say, and do
nothing that would displease God. Of course, he has often failed
(and is the first to admit it), but this man has such a heightened sense
of gratitude to God that he longs to show his love for him by
pleasing him in everything.

For about the last thirty years this longing to please God has
given him an amazing sense of God's presence with him all the
time. Probably because of this deep desire to show his love for
God, he has had a greater awareness than the rest of us of the fact
that *God is there.* You may say, "Well, of course God's there." But
how real is that to you? Is it much more than an article of faith?
For this brother—who, I must stress, claims to be no better than
the rest of us, just more blessed—it is the most important and
influential fact of existence. He is, quite simply, always with God.
And this presence gives him such joy that at times he has to take
steps to prevent his inward ecstasy from spilling over and embarrassing others.

It is true that his actual experience of God's presence varies in its intensity. Sometimes, usually when he is very busy at his daily work (he's a cook in a hospital kitchen), there are occasions when he becomes aware of the divine *absence*—not that God has gone away, but that he has forgotten that he is there, rather like a familiar friend or loved one who is sitting in the room with you while you are concentrating on something else.

What happens then, as he describes it, is that God "makes himself felt." As this happens—as though God were nudging him—he either silently lifts his heart to God in love and praise or, when circumstances make it possible without embarrassing other people, he actually puts it in words. One of his prayers on these occasions, he tells me, goes like this.

O my God,
Here I am.
All that I am is yours.
Make of me whatever you want.

Then it seems to him as if God, contented even with these few words, settles down again in the depth and center of his being.

Now I know that's a strange way to put it, but it is how he describes the experience, and I can confirm that in everyday life he certainly retains a vivid sense of God's nearness. So much so that he is now incapable of doubting the reality of it.

One obvious result of this (obvious to those of us who know him, that is) is this brother's air of total peace and contentment. Unlike the rest of us, he is not endlessly and restlessly searching for God, but has all the richness of God constantly available to him and enjoys him constantly.

I remember this brother giving an address in chapel one evening. Usually he is reluctant to talk about his experiences, but on this occasion he seemed so full of God he had to speak. He rebuked us—very gently and lovingly, let me add—for our blindness to the true riches that were within our grasp. He felt sorry for us (he said), who were like millionaires living on the old-age pension. "God has got so much to give," he said, "and yet we are content to pick up spiritual trifles. Our blindness and disobedience hinder him from working in our lives. They are like a dam built across a flowing stream, stopping its course and cutting off the life-giving supplies of water to the thirsty ground below.

"But when God finds a heart that is ready, open, and trusting, the obstacle is swept aside, and the pent-up waters flow as never before, surging into every corner and hidden place, bringing light and joy.

"We stop the current," he warned us, "mainly by the way we undervalue God's gifts. Simply to want him, above anything else, is the way to set the waters of life flowing.

"So—let us hold him back no longer. Let's break the dam that stops his blessings. Let's make a way for grace to flow, making up for the wasted, arid years of spiritual drought by clearing the gulleys and the gutters and letting the stream burst through.

"Let's enter into ourselves and root out all that holds back the river of God. We must keep at it, because not to advance, in the spiritual life, is to go back."

It was a moving talk, and I have passed it on to you hoping that you will do what we all did that night—compare his experience of God with your own, and let his words and example melt away any coolness of heart or failure of faith you may have experienced. I think our brother would want me to add that it is not at all a question of doing what he has done (as though he had achieved this state by his own efforts or merit), but of receiving, by faith, what he has received. The river flows wherever there is low land cleared ready before it. The thirsty land does nothing but drink up the goodness.

So let us both profit from this man's experience of God. He is not at all well-known, outside these four walls and the hospital kitchen, but he is known to God, as we are. Believe me, Richard, I have *personal knowledge* of all this—you may well have guessed already what I mean by that.

Yours in the Lord,
Laurie

Empty—to Be Filled

Dear Andrew,

I received two books and a letter this morning from Joan—you remember her? She helped us with our children's club a few years ago, when we were working in Springfield. Since then she has spent two years in a convent, and now she is preparing to make her profession as a nun. She particularly asked me to request your prayers for her, and also the prayers of your fellowship.

I feel she needs our prayers. It's a big step she is taking. We must pray that the motive for her renunciation of the world is the only right one, love of God alone, and that she is willing to devote herself wholly to him.

I was interested in the books she enclosed, and am sending one of them on to you. It deals with a subject that, in my opinion, sums up the whole business of living the spiritual life in the workaday world—the presence of God. As you must know by now, this is my hobby horse! I really do believe that the person who practices the presence of God will soon find his Christian life transformed.

One thing I have discovered—and this book, too, touches on it: if we are to practice God's presence truly, our hearts must be emptied of everything else. We cannot have the presence of God *and* an ambition for fame or money. We cannot have the presence of God *and* a love of luxury, or success, or prestige. I am not saying that only those without talents or without money can achieve the presence of God. I am saying that our desire must be first and foremost for him, with these other things taking the places he has allowed them to have in our lives. He cannot possess our hearts unless first he has emptied out the part that is already filled by someone or something else. And he cannot get to work in our hearts and do whatever he pleases there, until he is given all the room to work in.

But this is not a dry, negative, hard thing. It is not the end of pleasure, but its true beginning. For there is no life more delightful or satisfying than one spent in continual conversation with God, as anyone who has experienced it will testify. But let me add a warning: don't set out to practice the presence of God *in order* to obtain these joys and pleasures. It is God we seek, not delights and satisfactions. We long to be with him because we love him, not because he hands out good things to those who are nearest to him.

Sometimes I feel, Andrew, that if God had called me to be a preacher, I should preach on this subject every time I entered the pulpit. And if I were a spiritual counselor, I should urge everyone who came to see me to seek God instead. That's how important I believe it to be—and it is all so *simple*, too!

If we could glimpse for one moment the enormous need we have of God's grace and help, we should be unwilling to lose contact with him even for one second. We can't draw a single breath or lift a finger without him, much less fight spiritual battles and overcome the cunning and malice of the Evil One. It is high time we all resolved never willfully to forget him, and to spend the rest of our days in his presence. If we did, we should soon see the difference—in our own lives, and in our churches.

Pray for me, as I do for you.

Yours in Christ,
Laurie

The Danger of "Keeping the Rules"

Dear Tom,
Thanks for sending back those few articles—Mrs. Davies brought them in yesterday.

However, I was a bit surprised that you haven't yet made time to give me your thoughts on the little book I sent you a month ago. Did you receive it? I'm rather worried that you should ignore it, not because I sent it (after all, it's hardly the first book we've lent each other, is it?), but because the subject is terribly important. *Please*, Tom—read it, and start putting it into practice now, old as you are. Better late than never, as they say.

For myself, I simply do not understand how devout Christians like yourself can be satisfied with a religion that does not give them day by day the presence of God. After all, what else is there? In the depth of my being I keep myself shut away with him, even when I'm knee deep in vegetables! With him, I feel I can face anything. Without him, everything becomes unbearable.

This is a matter of mental, rather than bodily, discipline: though from time to time, of course, it is a good idea voluntarily to deprive ourselves of some completely innocent but perhaps distracting pleasure, simply to sharpen our attention on him, and show him that we are serious when we say we want him above everything else.

I don't mean by that that we should physically ill-treat ourselves, or go in for the sort of proud self-denial that St. Paul scorned (1 Col. 2:20-23). God's service is perfect freedom. We have to do our work, whatever it is, faithfully, without letting it dominate us or disturb our inward peace of mind. That in itself is a mental discipline, not spectacular, but demanding: to serve people, as God commands, and to keep in contact with him while we are doing it.

I know that you, Tom, are a great one for a "disciplined devotional life." You like to have rules, and keep them. But surely the danger is that the rules, and even the devotions, may cease to be means to an end—knowing God—and become an end *in themselves*. When, through practicing his presence, we are with God, who is our end, it is rather pointless to return to the means again. We can stay in his presence by expressing our love in any way that our spirits suggest—by prayer, by acts of thanksgiving, by doing our work to his glory, or by abstaining from some distracting luxury for a time. But by then we shall be in no danger at all of confusing the end with the means. We shall be in no danger of worshipping our own devotions!

Tom—I know you well enough (and you know me) to be able to say this. Time is running out. Persevere in seeking God, and his daily presence . . . and keep at it until your dying day. Pray for me, as I shall for you.

> Yours in the Lord,
> Laurie

He Wants So Little;
He Gives So Much

M y dear Gordon,
I was very touched by your letter, and can only say, I know how you
feel. I didn't realize you were past your three-score years, but I can
well remember the particular heart-searchings I went through at
about your time of life, and so I can sympathize. But there is nothing
so very special about being sixty-four, like you—or seventy-nine,
like me! What are years in a calendar to our God, with whom a
thousand of them are only one day?

I feel you should set out to make the most of your retirement, not
see it as the stage before the grave. Look at it this way: someone else
will have to worry now about your business, and you are free, with
time as never before, to enjoy drawing near to God. Until now the
daily pressure of earning your living has made it difficult for you to
have time—unhurried time—for him. Now that will be a problem
no longer, granted the will on your part to do it.

And it isn't hard work! He requires so little, and gives us so
much: a little remembering of him from time to time; a little lifting
up of the heart in praise; a brief offering to him of the joys and
sorrows of the moment—and he is there. Turn to him, Gordon,
all the time—when you are with friends, when you are enjoying
your meal: brief though your recognition of him is, he will accept
it, and he will come. He is so much nearer to us than we realize.

This doesn't mean you've got to spend your life in church, either!
We can make sanctuaries of our hearts and draw aside from time to
time within their quiet walls to talk with him. I believe that everyone—yes, *everyone*—is capable of this close, familiar relationship
with God, though perhaps not all equally . . . but that doesn't matter,
because he knows our capabilities. The important thing is to make
a start at it. He may be waiting for you to make *one* real and costly
decision to turn to him, and then it will all be easy.

Don't lose heart. We are both no longer young. Let's be determined to live and die with him. Nothing else really matters. Don't

get caught up in scrupulous observance of devotional rules or forms, but act as though you had confidence in God, as I know you have. Pray for me, as I do for you.

In Christ,
Laurie

Grasshopper Minds

My dear Robert,

I'm so glad you wrote to me about your problem of wandering thoughts in prayer. It is much more common than you think, but many devout Christians are unwilling to admit to it, in case it should appear that they were not as wholeheartedly devoted to God as they wish to appear.

The truth is, we all have grasshopper minds. We leap from thought to thought all the time. It is the hardest thing in the world to control our thoughts. But the will is still the master of our faculties, surely? Nothing can happen in our minds that is contrary to our wills. So the will must trap and subdue our thoughts, and carry them finally to the feet of Christ.

Mind you, once the bad habit of wandering thoughts has got a foothold, it is not easily dislodged. If over a long period our will has failed (or not tried very hard) to control our thoughts during times of prayer, even against our will, as it were, we may find our thoughts constantly being lured away to the things of the earth.

So, what can we do about it? You have already taken the first step: recognizing the need and sincerely wanting to do something to correct it. Certainly we shall confess this fault to God and humble ourselves before him, aware that to treat him casually is the final blasphemy against our Creator and Lord.

But is there any positive, practical advice I can give?

Well, I can offer one piece of negative advice! Don't pray long, wordy prayers. The longer and more wordy the prayer, the more likely our mind is to wander away from it. The same thing happens, after all, in a long and tedious conversation. God looks for quality, for intensity, rather than duration. It's not how long we pray that matters, but how sincerely and fervently. A rambling discourse on our knees is a certain recipe for wandering thoughts in our heads.

Instead, take the position in prayer before God of a dumb or helpless beggar at a rich man's gate. It is the beggar's responsibility to be alert to the rich man's moves. In the same way, make your times of prayer times of submission. Fix your thoughts on him, whether you speak or keep quiet. Watch for his every move.

Should you find that, even then, your mind has wandered, don't panic. To worry about it and make a great fuss just serves to heighten the problem and distract the mind still further. Quietly and calmly the will must reassert itself, briefly confessing the fault and then focusing the thoughts again on God. If you persevere at this—no matter if it happens twenty times in ten minutes—God will take pity on you, the distractions will become fewer, the mind will learn that it has a master in the will.

One way to improve mental concentration during prayer is to improve it at other times as well. It is a healthy exercise to practice control over wandering thoughts and daydreams through the day. Our minds should be constantly in the presence of God, and a conscious act of submission of our thoughts to him at intervals during the day will accustom us to center all our thoughts and desires on him. Prayer is not different from the other ingredients of living: it is really a concentrating and distilling of them before God. Our lives should be lived out before him—and if they are, then our times of prayer will not be so disastrously besieged by wandering and distracting thoughts.

I hope this helps. Above all, don't be discouraged. The heart is deceitful above all things, but God understands our frailty . . . he remembers that we are "only dust."

In Christ,
Laurie

Put Your Heart with Your Treasure

My dear John,

Would you pass on the enclosed note to Miss Bennett? She wrote me a long letter, full of questions and requests for advice, but I do not have her address, so I'm asking you to act as my mailman.

Miss Bennett seems to me to have excellent intentions, but little patience. She tries to run faster than grace. I have tried to tell her, very gently, that one does not become holy all at once, whatever some enthusiastic Christians may say. We must learn to walk before we can run.

Let me know how she gets on, from time to time, won't you? I'm sure she will be fervent, but hope she will also be obedient.

After all, our chief ambition in life should be to please God, and we can only do that by obeying him. Everything else is folly and unreality. You and I have walked with him, John, for over forty years. Have we made the best use of them? Have we used them to love and serve God, who in his mercy has called us to himself for that very purpose? For myself, I must admit I am very ashamed when I contrast his wonderful goodness and kindness to me, not only in the past but also today, with my grudging and inadequate love and service, and my slow progress on the path to "the perfect man."

Well, all is not lost. We have a little time left, by his mercy. It isn't too late for us to make up for lost time and return to God, the "Father of mercies," who is always ready to welcome us back. It isn't too late to renounce, for love of him, all that is not consistent with that love, and to train our minds to think of him constantly. I have no doubt that, if we do, the results will exceed our wildest hopes.

As I see it, John, we cannot even hope to escape the spiritual dangers that surround us in the modern world without the actual and *continual* help and grace of God. Without it, we can do nothing but sin. With it, we can do "all things." So—let's pray for his grace continually.

Yet, how can we pray to him without being with him, in his presence? And how can we be with him without thinking of him often? And how can we often think of him unless we form a habit of doing so? These things don't just happen!

I know what you are thinking to yourself as you read this—"Dear old Laurie, back on his hobby horse again!" Well, I admit it, I do harp on it, but only because it is true—this is the best, and easiest, and most effective method I know of cultivating the presence of God. I have used it for many years, and can only recommend it to everybody else.

After all, we must know someone before we can love him. In order to know God, we must think of him. And when we think of him, our love will grow, because our hearts will be where our treasure is.

Forgive me for playing an old record again and again! Yet you know how much this means to me, and how anxious I am that everybody should share in it.

Yours in him,
Laurie

Priorities

Dear Philip and Mary,

You really put me on the spot! I've delayed writing to your friend Martin all week, and have only got down to it now because I simply could not refuse a request from such old and dear friends as you. I'm enclosing a letter to him—would you address the envelope and forward it to him? You didn't give me his address. I'm delighted to know of your own trust and confidence in God. It's a fact, isn't it, that we just can't have too much of so good and faithful a friend, who will never let us down—in this world, or the next.

Which brings me to Martin's problem. I can quite understand how upset he is over the way his human friend has let him down. Our Lord, too, knew what it was to be forsaken by his friends when he needed them most. It is a common enough human experience, because fallen men and women *are* unreliable. We give someone a part of ourselves when we give them our friendship. We take a risk. Naturally, it hurts when they prove to be fickle, selfish, or untrustworthy.

What Martin needs to do (though it is easier said than done) is to turn this loss to his own advantage, by putting all his confidence again in *God*. He is a far more powerful and more reliable friend than any man or woman. But, more than that, he changes our circumstances as he pleases. It may well be that he has another human friend for Martin, far better and more reliable than the one he has lost.

Perhaps Martin was *too* attached to his friend. It is right to love our friends, of course—but without trespassing on the love of God, which must take first place.

We can, in fact, learn a great deal about the love of God from the way we treat our friends. For example, it would be very discourteous to invite a friend to our home and then leave him to sit alone in a corner while we go ahead with our own activities, ignoring him completely. Yet that is what we do with God. We have invited him, in his Son, to enter our hearts and live there—but often we neglect him, almost forgetting that he is there at all, so distracted are we by other things and other people.

The Christian's biggest, most important job on earth is to live and die with the Lord. He can hardly do that if the slightest diversion drives all thoughts of God out of his mind. It is all a question of priorities, really.

> Yours in the Lord,
> Laurie

Sweetness in Suffering

Mrs. Marion Jones
Surgical Ward
Massachusetts General Hospital

Dear Marion,

I have had you on my mind ever since our fellowship meeting at lunch time today, when Lois told us of your condition and several of your friends prayed very movingly for your recovery, or the relief of your pain. I hope you will forgive my writing to you, but I believe God wants me to do this and I can get no peace of mind until I do his will.

You see, I could not really and truly join in their prayers for you—not that I doubt either their sincerity or their faith, and certainly not that I am indifferent to your suffering, but because I have learned, through the small burdens of pain that I have had to bear, a different and (dare I suggest) a better way to please God in times of illness.

I have been thinking how to say this. It is simply that I would rather we concentrated our prayers on *you*, rather than your suffering. Let me explain.

I am sure you accept the fact that God has permitted you to suffer in this way. If he is truly *King*, then this illness could not have come to you against his will. I believe (with the Epistle to the Hebrews, chapter twelve) that such things come to us from the hand of God, as a means that he uses to make us more completely his, and that rightly accepted and borne they bring great sweetness and consolation into our lives. This illness is not, then, an enemy to be fought, but an ally in the spiritual warfare to be gladly received and used.

So take strength from this: Christ holds you fastened to this cross, and Christ will release you from it when he thinks fit. In either case, it is obviously better to be held by him—on or off a cross—than to be apart from him.

Of course, you can't expect those who do not believe in God to see things in this way. You cannot ask an unbeliever to suffer as a

Christian. He considers illness as an enemy of life and nature, and finds nothing in it but grief and distress. The Christian, however, sees it as coming from the hands of God. This is the crucial difference.

I hope you can discover for yourself that God is often—at least, in some sense—nearer to us in sickness than in health. To put all our hope and faith into *recovery* is almost like saying we want to have less of him. Instead, we should put our faith and hope *in him*. After all, even the medical treatment you receive and the drugs you are given will only succeed so far as he permits. Perhaps he is reserving your complete cure to himself, and waiting only for you to commit yourself into his hands without question.

I expect you are saying to yourself—"That's all right for *him*." But, truthfully, however happy you may think I am at this moment, I envy you. To suffer *with my God* is not pain, but paradise. To "enjoy myself" without him would be hell. I must, very shortly (weeks, months, years—who knows?) go to God. What comforts me here and now is that I can see him and know him by faith. But then I shall believe no more. I shall *see*. So—as St. Paul himself put it—"for me to live is Christ, and to die is gain." Anything—life, joy, pain, death—that brings me nearer to him cannot be bad.

Keep close to God. I shall ask him to be with you.

Yours, because his,
Laurie

The Offering of Pain

Mrs. Marion Jones
Surgical Ward
Massachusetts General Hospital

My dear Marion,
I have had you very much in my thoughts and prayers since I last

wrote to you a couple of weeks ago. I have a little idea of how much you must be suffering, and I want you to know that I did *not* mean that suffering was unimportant or easily borne, even with God's help. What I was trying to say was that if we are accustomed to live in the presence of God, and if we believe that everything that comes to us comes with his permission, then those two facts will help to alleviate our suffering. God often permits us to suffer a little to lead us on to maturity, and to drive us into his arms.

So, offer him your pains. They come from him, or by his permission, so turn them into an offering to lay at his feet—his will for you accepted and carried through. Ask him for the strength you will need to bear them. And, above all, continually lift your thoughts away from the pain you feel and toward him, who loves you as a Father loves his favorite child. God has many ways of drawing us to himself. Sometimes his way is to hide himself from us for a time. It is then, most of all, that faith, and faith *only*, will support us and give a firm foundation to our confidence in him.

I have no idea what God may have in store for me, of pleasure or of pain. All I know is—and sometimes it almost makes me feel guilty—that in a world where suffering faces us on every side, I, who deserve only to be punished by God, feel such a continual joy in him that at times I can hardly stop myself from shouting and rejoicing from the rooftops!

Dear Marion, I would willingly ask God for a part of your pain, if that would help—but I know my weakness, and know that without his continual presence I should be unable to bear it. But I also know that he has promised never to leave me. Let us resolve never to leave him. Let us live and die in his presence.

Pray for me as I promise to pray for you.

                    Yours in him,
                    Laurie

In the Hands of God

Mrs. Marion Jones
Surgical Ward
Massachusetts General Hospital

My dear Marion,

It hurts me to see you suffer. Since I saw you last week, I have had you constantly in my thoughts and in my prayers. The only relief I can find is to reassure myself that God must love you very much to permit you to suffer so much. He must also be very confident of your love for him. "The Lord disciplines those whom he *loves* . . ."

However, I have another particular reason for writing. You remember we were talking last week about "putting God to the test"—the danger of asking God to do miraculously what we are well able to do, in his strength, without a miracle. We were especially talking about healing, and I argued that it was right to use human medicine and medical skills, because they, too, were given by God, rather than seek a sort of spiritual shortcut by asking for direct divine healing.

But as I have thought and prayed about you, I have come to feeling that the moment is now passed when you could be expected to rely on ordinary medical care. You know this, so it is not cruel to put it into words: humanly speaking, your case is hopeless. You have endured for months the often painful investigations and treatments prescribed by your doctors. You have had surgery, chemotherapy, cobalt therapy, and just about everything else—and you have accepted it all patiently, and cooperated with those who have taken care of you.

But you are no better. In fact, as you yourself realize, you are getting weaker every day.

In such circumstances, I wonder whether it might not be right for you to have a talk with your doctor, and say to him that you appreciate very much all that has been done for you, and the thought and devotion that has gone into your treatment, but, as it doesn't seem to be achieving anything, you would now prefer to be left in the hands of God. It would not, I'm sure, be "tempting God" to resign yourself with perfect trust into his hands, for healing, if that is his will; or for a quiet and peaceful path into his presence, if that is what he desires for you.

I do not mean, of course, that you should reject all medical care, or that such a course rules out your receiving drugs or other treatment that will lessen your pain. I simply mean that the moment may have come when your chief concern should cease to be human remedies, and start to be a total and trusting dependence on the providence of God. That is not to say that you have not been trusting him all along. But you have, up to now, been looking for him to help you *through human agents* (your doctors and nurses). Now, perhaps, he wants you to expect everything *from him.* In a sense, this is simply to make a virtue out of a necessity. Human help—skillful and dedicated though it may be—cannot meet your needs. Turn, then, to God, and comfort yourself with him, the only Physician who fully understands and can completely cure every sickness of body and spirit.

I know it is hard to pray for strength to bear pain, rather than for the pain to be taken away. But love sweetens pain—think of a mother in childbirth. And when one loves God, and feels his warm answering love, pain *is* sweetened. He loves us beyond our wildest imagination. Let him prove his promises.

Always yours in our Lord,
Laurie

Heaven's Threshold

Mrs. Marion Jones
Surgical Ward
Massachusetts General Hospital

My dear Marion,

I was so glad to hear from you, though your letter took rather a long time to reach me! Since I saw you I've been rather ill myself, and had the opportunity to test the advice I had been giving you. In fact, I think I can say I've been "at death's door" once or twice recently—and, as I expected, never felt nearer God than when standing on the threshold of heaven.

I am so thankful to God for the news that you are feeling better and that he has drawn nearer to you as you have been drawn nearer to him. I have always believed, and am more sure than ever now, that it is paradise to suffer with him, but hell to be at ease without him. So that, if we want to discover the peace of paradise on earth, we must get used to living in constant communication with him. In this relationship the familiarity (we know him so well) will be balanced by our humility (because it is staggering to think that *he* should want to be with *us*), with love the keynote of it all.

More than that, we must guard our affections, like a faithful husband or wife, keeping them for him and making sure that we are not seduced by any earthly distraction. We must convert the inner sanctuary of our affections into a spiritual temple where he is constantly worshipped. And we must check ourselves—our actions, attitudes, and words—continually, to see that we are not displeasing him. If we do these things, heaven is already here, and suffering is robbed of its bitter bite.

I realize that it is difficult, at least at first, to follow this path. Our instinct is to shrink from pain and suffering—and hide ourselves from God. The core of the difficulty, however, is not the presence of pain, but the absence of *faith*. We find it very hard to believe that God knows all, and therefore that what he plans for us is best. We prefer to follow our fallen reason, or our own defective sight. But "we walk by faith, not by sight" (2 Cor. 5:7). What we can see, and what we can understand is very, very limited. God knows and sees *all*.

So, although it *is* difficult, it is not impossible. I have proved that. God never refuses his grace to those who ask for his help sincerely—and the chief part of that grace is the gift of faith to trust him. Knock at his door, and keep on knocking—and I promise you that in his own good time God will open to you and give you everything that he has been waiting to give you for many years.

I am at his door now, and expecting him at any moment. Pray for me, Marion, as I do for you.

Laurie

One Simple Act

Mrs. Marion Jones
Surgical Ward
Massachusetts General Hospital

My dear Marion,
God knows what we really need, and all he does is for the best. If only we could grasp how much he loves us, we should be more ready to receive with trusting joy both the bitter and the sweet from his hand. All we must know is that it comes from him . . . and this he has assured us. Pain is only intolerable when seen in a distorted light. But when we know it is the hand of a loving God that shapes it all, and that it is our Father who gives us the cup of sorrow to drink, there is no distortion and so no unbearable burden.

We should concentrate on knowing God. The more we know him, the more we shall long to know him better. Love without knowledge (like a man infatuated with the photograph of a beautiful girl) is shallow and superficial; but the deeper our knowledge, the deeper and more satisfying our love. If our love of God is based on knowledge, we shall love him equally in pain or pleasure.

Many Christians seem to feel that the way to get "near" to God is to seek experience of him—special gifts and sensations of the Holy Spirit. But it seems to me that such experiences, however moving, cannot bring us as near God as faith does in one simple act! After all, he is not far away. He is *within* us. We have no need to look for him anywhere else. Wouldn't it be regarded as foolish, and even wrong, to go off in search of the good, when the best is being offered to us?

So let us seek the best, and the best is his presence with us all day long. Let us reject all substitutes for this. If we take only one hesitant step toward him, he will come to meet us.

Forgive me—I didn't mean to preach a sermon! I'm delighted to hear of the way God has comforted and relieved you. To him be the thanks and the glory.

For my part, I hope to have the joy of seeing him any day now. Let us pray for one another.

Yours in the Lord,
Laurie

Epilogue: God Is Our Goal

A few days after writing that last letter to Marion Jones, Brother Lawrence was taken seriously ill, and within a week he had died. So ended a life that, though carried on in humble circumstances and completely without publicity, was exceptional for its honesty, quality, and knowledge of God. Just before he retired from the hospital S.D. kitchen, a member of our fellowship asked Laurie to sum up what his faith meant in terms of his daily work. This was his reply.

"You all know that soon after my conversion at the age of eighteen I set myself to make God the goal of all my thoughts and desires. To help toward this, I spent the hours appointed in our Community for private prayer thinking of God, so as to convince my mind of his real and actual existence and let that truth impress itself deeply on my heart. I did this, let me say, not by elaborate intellectual processes (which would be beyond me), nor by complicated schemes of meditation, but by opening my mind and then my heart to the light of faith. The result of this, as I have often tried to explain, was an overwhelming sense of the reality of God's presence, and I resolved never to forget him or neglect him again. In fact, I have often failed; but he always welcomes me back again when I confess my failure and turn once more to him.

"On a normal, working day, I would try to fill my waking mind with thoughts of God—in his infinite power, and in his personality. The Bible often began my thinking, and prayer always filled this out and made it personal to me.

"So, by the time I set off to work, I had already been in God's presence for an hour or so—not just on my knees, you must understand, but while I had been shaving and eating my breakfast, too.

"When I got to the kitchen I would check on the day's menus, assignments, special diets, delivery schedules, and so on. Then, having got a picture of the day's work, I would briefly but deliberately commit it to God. I often used the same prayer:

O my God, you are always with me. Since I must now, in obedience to your will for me, apply my mind to my day's work, grant me the grace I shall need to continue through it in your presence. Help me to do this work to your glory. Receive it as a spiritual offering. And let my desire be only to please you.

"Then, as the day's routine began, I would know that I was as near God, and he as near me, as if I could have seen him there with my physical eyes.

"At the end of the day I would stop to think about how it had gone. If things had gone well, both in my work and in my consciousness of God, I would give him thanks. If it had not gone well, I would ask his forgiveness and, without allowing myself to become discouraged by failure, would set my mind right again and turn once more to thinking of God as if I had never stopped. So I can honestly say that, through years of practice, I have come to a condition where it would be as difficult for me not to think of God, as it used to be to get into the habit of doing so."

Not surprisingly, in view of the tremendous blessing Laurie obtained from his walk with God, he would often urge the rest of us to seek God in the same kind of way. This might have been embarrassing or annoying. But in fact his own life was a stronger argument for his cause than any words he could find. Just to look at him was to be convinced—his face radiated joy and calmness, no matter how hectic the day.

In fact, it was this that impressed people most of all about him. The Special Diets kitchen was often very busy, and usually understaffed. The phone seemed to ring incessantly, and yet people expected the meals to arrive on the wards at the exact time scheduled. But, in the busiest moments, with noises, heat, and tempers getting a bit frayed at the edges, Laurie remained calm— and close to God.

It wasn't that he wandered through it all with a sort of distant, "spiritual" look on his face, remote from us lesser mortals. That would be a hopelessly wrong picture. It was just that panic (on the one hand) or laziness (on the other) were totally foreign to him. He was serving God, and that would be best done by being calm, composed . . . and hard-working. He saw no hint of contradiction in those attitudes.

"After all," he once said to me, "the times when I am working and the times when I am praying are no different in *kind*. In the noise and clutter of the kitchen, with half a dozen people screaming for different things at once, I can possess the peace of God, and know the God of peace, as truly as if I were on my knees at the altar rail."

The Imitation of Christ
Thomas à Kempis

retold by Bernard Bangley

Introduction

I first encountered *The Imitation of Christ* in 1947. Our pastor had given a copy to my brother as a high school graduation present. He never read it.

I tried to read it, but the English of the "revised translation" seemed archaic and virtually meaningless to my young mind. It may have been a treasure chest, but it was firmly locked and barred.

That little book found its way onto my shelves and followed me around until my forty-fourth year—a year of overwhelming stress and conflict. At no other time in my life have I been more aware of my human frailty and my total dependence upon God. I had some tough professional decisions to make, values to sort out, priorities to establish, and responsibilities to shoulder. The time was ripe for me to discover personally the tremendous value of that little purple book I had been carrying around for more than thirty years. I had, by now, read widely enough so that the language was no longer a barrier to my understanding, and I had gained maturity enough for the concepts to make sense. To my astonishment, the thing lived and breathed! Day after day the messages of its brief chapters reached into the very heart of things, took the world as I had found it to be and said something entirely rational and deeply spiritual about it. My own thinking was clarified and confirmed. I found in these pages wisdom and courage "for the facing of this hour . . . for the living of these days."

I read *The Imitation* under a variety of circumstances during the working day. I read it slowly, prayerfully. I marked it with a pencil, and copied portions of it to share with my wife. Sometimes, in my enthusiasm, I would telephone her and read a gem of a sentence I had just discovered. It was unbelievable how close the book's guidance came to my personal situation, how applicable its insights were to my professional dilemma. I can think of no better way to express it than to say that God met me in those pages. The prayers of the book prompted a profound inner response of prayer in me. God and I *communicated*.

Sometimes I was so startled by what I had read that I gave a little gasp of astonishment. How could anybody speak across all those centuries to my specific need with such clarity and certainty? These words were never intended for me; they were written by a monk to inspire and instruct those inside a monastery. And yet, the original author wrote with such genuine humanity, with such sincerity and insight into godliness, that the book has become the common possession of us all. It contains no barrier of time or place, no denominational narrowness. The words are sparks from the anvil of intense personal experience and they ignite spontaneous fires in the hearts of readers who recognize their own spiritual struggles. God, through these brief pages, has given us something pure and simple that drives straight to the heart of the only thing that really matters—our relationship with God and God's creation.

Such a discovery cries out to be shared. I highly recommended it to others. A few attempted to find in it what I had seen, but most could not seem to catch my enthusiasm. The available translations just didn't read easily enough for the average person in today's world. There were so many barriers of style to overcome. The book was like a black walnut: delicious meat concealed in a hard, unyielding shell.

I knew what my task was. After studying English translations and an edition in the original Latin, I began to rewrite, in my own language, certain pages of the great classic. To my delight, this process worked. There was nothing out of date in the author's understanding of people and God. All that was needed to make it accessible to modern readers was fresh expression. The task became a labor of love.

I should make it clear that you are not holding a literal translation of De Imitatione Christi. My purpose has been to communicate. I have tried to use language that clearly conveys the meaning and intent of the original while avoiding some of the traps inherent in a more literal rendering. For instance, when we are urged to have "contempt of ourselves," this is not an invitation to wallow in the depths of self-hatred and despair about ourselves, a thing alien to the life of Christ. Rather, the child of God is called upon to have a realistic estimation of himself as a person. What is meant by "contempt" in this case is something far more essential to the Christian life; I have called it "a humble opinion of ourselves."

In Book I, Chapter XV, the author agrees with Seneca in saying that it is better to avoid society. "As often as I have been among men, I have returned home less a man." While seeing his point, I am not convinced that we see Christ demonstrate such an attitude. Jesus certainly escaped the crowds by retreating to lonely mountaintops, but only for brief periods. He did this in order to restore himself so that he could wade back into the masses to minister. Our Lord was at his best when in conversation with other people. In the same vein, Chapter VIII encourages us to avoid social contact. "Don't converse too much with young people and strangers . . . Be friends with God and his angels, and avoid the acquaintance of men." All of this needs to be understood in the context of the book's original monastic setting, but it hardly offers Christian counsel today. I have, therefore, omitted these pages from the present edition.

The original audience was obviously male. For today's readers I have rendered such phrases as "My son," with the neuter, "My child." In places, I have paraphrased freely. In other places, I have omitted some of the original's parallelisms or dropped out a repetitious paragraph. While this may result in a loss of some of the cumulative impact of reading *The Imitation* in its original form, the streamlining makes it move along faster for modern readers. Such editing has been done with care and discretion, and never with the intention of twisting this beautiful classic into a new shape.

The original contains a generous sprinkling of quotations from, and allusions to, Holy Scripture. I have allowed the allusions to pass without pointing them out. Direct quotations appear within quotation marks and are taken from the *Good News Bible (Today's English Version)*, published by the American Bible Society. In a few instances, where the original quotes only a fragment of a verse, I have included the entire verse.

The title of Thomas à Kempis's work has almost lost meaning to modern readers. Because the word turns up so frequently on supermarket shelves, "imitation" has come to mean "artificial." But the Latin *imitatio* means imitating or copying in the sense of *following* Christ. Of course, none of us can live a duplicate of the Perfect Life, but we can pattern our lives after Christ's in our own way. We know that Jesus Christ is far more than an excellent model for good living. He is the Son of God, our Savior. But once we have made that great affirmation of faith, we must begin inward growth that reflects our Lord's image. And it is in expressing the things we believe by the things we do that this little book offers its unsurpassed counsel.

Reading through these pages you will naturally want to know more about the origin and history of this Christian classic. (I've included background information in the Afterword to satisfy your curiosity.) In the five centuries of its existence it has appeared in about six thousand editions worldwide. Only the Bible has been translated into more languages. *The Imitation of Christ* has been read and appreciated by many of the greatest people in history, and by countless millions of less famous Christians and seekers—a number that continues to grow with each new generation. And now you are among them.

As you begin reading *The Imitation*, you step into a very special world, a world that seems curiously out of joint. The values it holds before us are not dear to a society based on selfish ambition. However, they may well be the perfect antidote to some of the poisonous ideas that currently infect our planet. Of this I have no doubt: the advice works. These pages are not merely quaint reminders of a bygone era. I believe the teachings were as radically opposed to popular values in the fourteenth century as they are to the values of today. Here is a human dynamic that remains forever true. When we are told where to find peace, or the route to misery, we are given an accurate road map, honestly labeled.

"There is a gentle eloquence in *The Imitation*," wrote Will Durant, "that echoes the profound simplicity of Christ's sermons and parables. It is an ever needed check on the intellectual pride of frail reason and shallow sophistication. When we are weary of facing our responsibilities in life we shall find no better refuge than Thomas à Kempis's Fifth Gospel."

PART I

Valuable Advice
for Spiritual Living

How to Follow Christ
and Disregard the
World's Prizes

The Lord says, "Whoever follows me will never walk in darkness" (John 8:12). Christ encourages us to pattern our lives after his so we can become spiritually enlightened. Our most important task, then, is to meditate on the life of Jesus Christ.

Christ's teaching is superior to all the teachings of the saints, and if you have the Spirit you will discover through him "the hidden manna" of the Word (Rev. 2:17). Many who have heard the gospel all their lives have not been affected by it because they do not have Christ's Spirit. If you truly want to understand and enjoy the words of Christ, you must attempt to live like him.

What is the point of scholarly discussion of a deep subject like the Trinity, if you lack humility? You can be sure that profound talk does not make anyone holy and just, but a pure life pleases God. I would rather feel contrition than know its definition!

If you knew the entire Bible by heart and were familiar with all the philosophers, what good would it all be without the love of God and his grace?

Anything other than loving and serving God is "meaningless, meaningless . . . utterly meaningless" (Eccles. 1:2).

Here is the wisest thing you can do: forget the world and seek the things of heaven.

It is pointless, then, to desire and trust perishable wealth.

It is also pointless to search after honors or to be a social climber.

It is useless to give in to physical desires, and to crave wrong things when indulging ourselves will only bring severe punishment.

It is futile to wish for a long life and then to give so little care to living well.

It is nothing but vanity to think only of this present life and to ignore the future.

It is vain to care about things that are quickly passing away rather than to hurry to the place of everlasting joy.

Repeat this proverb frequently: "The eye never has enough nor the ear its fill of hearing" (Eccles. 1:8). Try, then, to turn your heart away from the love of things that can be seen, and to start loving the things that cannot be seen. Those who follow the way of sensuality will have a nagging conscience and lose God's favor.

Have a Humble Opinion of Yourself

It is natural for all of us to desire knowledge, but what is the value of knowledge without respect for God? The most ordinary person who serves God is better than a proud philosopher who neglects himself while studying the stars. If you really know yourself, you will see that nothing about yourself is worthy of praise. "If . . . I can fathom all mysteries and all knowledge . . . but have not love, I am nothing" (1 Cor. 13:2). When I stand in God's presence, I am judged by the things I do.

Great learning can be a distraction; it can make you try to appear wise in order to win praise. There are many things you can know that will be of little value to your soul, and it is not wise to waste your time on them. Words do not nourish the soul, but a life well-lived brings comfort to the mind. A clear conscience will give you confidence before God.

If you think you know a lot about something, remind yourself that there are many more things you do not know. "Do not be proud, but be willing to associate with people of low position. Do not be conceited" (Rom. 12:16). If you want to learn something worthwhile, learn how to be a nobody.

The most profound and valuable lesson of all is to know yourself truly and to have a humble opinion of yourself.

Think well of others. If you see someone else engaging in a sinful act or crime, do not let that make you think more highly of yourself. You do not know how long it may be before you also stumble. All of us are frail; consider yourself no stronger than anyone else!

True Education

"Blessed is the man you discipline, O LORD, the man you teach from your law" (Ps. 94:12).

Our opinions and senses frequently mislead us. "What do we gain from all our work? . . . He has given us a desire to know the future, but never gives us the satisfaction of fully understanding what he does" (Eccles. 3:9, 11, Good News Bible). We won't be held responsible for this ignorance.

O God of truth, unite me with yourself in everlasting love. I am tired of reading and hearing many things. All I desire is you. Silence all teachers.

Let every creature be hushed reverently in your presence. Speak to me intimately.

The more a person is in harmony with himself and the more simple he is inwardly, the more he understands intuitively. He receives divine illumination.

A pure, honest, and stable spirit is not distracted by a lot of activity. He does everything to honor God and is at rest within himself. He seeks to be free from all selfishness.

A good, devout person considers inwardly the things he intends to do outwardly. Who has a greater struggle than one who tries to overcome himself? And this is our job—to work at conquering ourselves, to become stronger each day, and to make a little progress toward goodness.

Even our best efforts have imperfections, and all of our thinking includes some stupidity. A humble understanding of ourselves is a more certain way to God than the most in-depth study.

But learning is not to be condemned! Knowledge is good. It is God's gift to us. However, a clear conscience and a decent life are superior to it. The fruitless error comes in desiring to know much, rather than to live well.

If we were as careful in weeding out vices and planting virtues as we are in scholarly research, we would not have so much evil and scandal among us, or so much carelessness in religious houses.

You can be certain of this: when the day of Judgment comes, we shall not be asked what we have read, but what we have done; not how well we have spoken, but how well we have lived.

Tell me, where now are all the great doctors and masters you used to know? Others sit in their offices, and the former ones already are forgotten. See how soon this world's glory fades!

Authentic greatness is found in great love.

He is genuinely great who considers himself small and cares nothing about high honors.

I am truly wise if I look upon all earthly things "as [garbage], that I may gain Christ" (Phil. 3:8).

And the most learned of all is he who does the will of God while denying himself.

Prudent Living

We should not be too credulous. We need to consider carefully everything we hear. We should spend time in thought before God. Sadly, we are so weak that we frequently believe and repeat ugly rumors rather than good things. It is best not to accept every report. Human beings have a tendency to evil, and even the most reliable sources make mistakes.

"It is not good to have zeal without knowledge, nor to be hasty and miss the way" (Prov. 19:2). In a similar manner, don't believe everything you hear. Don't be quick to pour it into others' ears.

The more humility you have and the more subject you are to God, the wiser you will be, and the more at peace.

Reading the Bible

Look for truth in the Bible, not eloquence. Every verse should be read in the spirit with which it was written.

Read the devout and simple books as gladly as the learned and profound. Don't worry about the author's authority or his level of education. Allow the love of simple truth to attract you. Don't ask, "Who said this?" Instead, pay attention to what is said. People die, but God's Word will never pass away.

Sometimes our curiosity interferes with our Bible reading. We want to discuss and understand parts we should simply pass by.

If you want to make your Scripture reading worthwhile, read with humility, simplicity, and faith. Don't try to appear learned. Listen in silence to the words of the holy men, and take pleasure in the teachings of the elders. They spoke with good reason.

Controlling Excess Desire

If you want something obsessively, you will be restless within yourself. The arrogant and the greedy can never relax. It is the poor and the spiritually humble who know what peace is.

If you are not yet able to deny yourself, you will be easily tempted. Small, insignificant things will make you their slave.

The spiritually weak prefer sensuality and are not able to give up earthly desires completely. That's why they are sad when they must abandon something and easily angered when opposed.

Suppose you get something you want. Soon you may be remorseful to have that thing. Surrendering to your passions will not help you find peace. Only by resisting them can you be truly at peace.

There is simply no peace in the heart of a person who lives an animal existence or who places all importance on outward things. Peace is reserved for the sincerely spiritual person.

Taking Charge

Be free! Master yourself! Make sure that all things are under you, and that you are not under them. Don't be a slave to anything. Be free!

Pride and Humility

"The Lord says, 'I will condemn the person who turns away from me and puts his trust in man, in the strength of mortal man' " (Jer. 17:5, Good News Bible).

Do not be ashamed to serve others because of your love for Jesus Christ, or to appear poor in the world's eyes.

Do not count on your own strength; trust God. Do what you can, and God will supply the difference.

"Let not the wise man boast of his wisdom, or the strong man boast of strength, or the rich man boast of his riches" (Jer. 9:23).

"Clothe yourselves with humility toward one another, because, 'God opposes the proud but gives grace to the humble' " (1 Pet. 5:5).

Take glory neither in money, if you have some, nor in influential friends, but in God who gives you everything and above all wants to give you himself.

Avoid boasting about the size or beauty of your body, which a little illness can disfigure or destroy.

Have no pride in your native wit and talent; that would displease God who gave you every good thing that you naturally possess.

Reject the thought that you are better than anyone else. If you think such haughty thoughts, God (who knows what is in you) will consider you worse than they.

Pride about our good deeds is pointless. God has his own ideas regarding what is good and he does not always agree with us. If there is anything good about you, believe better things of others. This will keep you humble.

It will not hurt you at all to consider yourself less righteous than others, but it will be disastrous for you to consider yourself better than even one person.

The humble are always at peace; the proud are often envious and angry.

Subjection in the Lord

It is of great importance to be obedient, to respect authority, and to let someone else captain our ship. It is far safer to follow than to lead.

Yes, most people want to manage things their own way. But if God is among us, it is sometimes necessary to surrender our personal opinion in order to keep harmony.

Who is intelligent enough to know everything? Don't be too sure of yourself. Be willing to hear what others think. Sometimes, even if you have a good idea, it is better to discard it in favor of another, for God's sake. It is less dangerous to take advice than to give it.

Perhaps your opinion is just as good as anyone's. But if you stubbornly refuse to yield to others when there is a good reason or a just cause to do so, all you prove is your obstinate pride.

Guarding the Mouth

Avoid small talk as much as you can. Even shop talk can be a great hindrance. Sometimes I wish I had remained silent, that I had not spoken in a crowd.

Our chattering is an escape from unwelcome thinking. We keep the conversation on comfortable subjects. Small comfort! Sometimes it even robs us of inward consolation.

Watch and pray, so that you won't waste your time. If you want to talk about something, discuss a worthwhile subject.

Failing to guard your mouth is a very bad habit. But reverent discussion of spiritual matters can help us all grow, especially when the group that is gathered is unified in God.

Finding Peace

We will have much peace if we refrain from minding the business of others.

Those with a unity of purpose are blessed with such peace.

Do you know why some of the saints were so genuine and contemplative? It was because they worked hard at being free from earthly desires. This allowed them to move closer to God and to develop their inner life freely.

We are enslaved too much by our emotions, and we worry too much about transitory things.

Only occasionally do we win out over even one vice, and no desire burns within us to improve daily the quality of our behavior. That is why we continue to be apathetic and cold. If we could overcome ourselves, and not be all mixed up in our hearts, then we would be delighted with spiritual things and have a little experience with heavenly contemplation.

Our main problem—our *only* problem—is that we are caught in a spider's web of passions and lusts, and have no desire for a higher way. When even a minor problem comes up, we are immediately discouraged and turn to earthly kinds of comforts.

But if we try to be brave and stand firm in the battle, God will certainly help us. He presents us with the challenge and stands ready to assist us. All we need to do is trust his free gift of grace and we will win.

We would be well on the way to perfection if we could weed out one vice from ourselves each year. But we often find that we were better persons just after our conversion than we are after many years of being a Christian. Every day that passes should make us more like Christ, but we tend to grow cooler rather than warmer.

If we would make big demands on ourselves at the beginning, we would find it easier going later on. It is a hard job to quit old habits, and it is even more difficult to resist our own desires. But if you can't handle small things, how will you deal with big ones?

Put up a fight right at the beginning. Break a bad habit. Otherwise, it may draw you by small steps you never notice into greater difficulty.

If you had any idea how much inward peace you would gain for yourself, and how much joy you would bring to others by devoting yourself singleheartedly to God, you would certainly pay more attention to your spiritual progress.

The Value of Adversity

Sometimes it is good for us to have trouble and crosses to bear. Adversity can return us to our senses. It can remind us that we are here as refugees, and that we must not place our trust in anything belonging to the world.

It is good that people sometimes misunderstand us, that they have a poor opinion of us even when our intentions are good. Such experiences lead toward humility and protect us from conceit. Under trying circumstances we seek God all the more. Our inner life grows stronger when we are outwardly condemned.

If you will fully establish yourself in God, you will not need the consolation of others. When we are troubled with temptation and evil thoughts, then we see clearly the great need we have of God, since without him we can do nothing good. Then with weariness and sorrow we may "desire to depart and be with Christ" (Phil 1:23), for we understand that absolute security and peace do not exist in this world.

How to Resist Temptation

As long as we live in this world, we will endure trials and temptation. As it is written in Job,

"Does not man have hard service on earth?
Are not his days like those of a hired man?
Like a slave longing for the evening shadows,
or a hired man his wages" (Job 7:1-2).

Be careful, therefore, about your own temptations. Pray about them. "Be alert, be on the watch! Your enemy, the Devil, roams around like a roaring lion, looking for someone to devour" (1 Pet.

5:8). No one is so good that he is immune to temptation; we will never be entirely free of it.

Still, temptation can be a service to us. It may be a burden, but it can bring us humility and teach us good lessons. All of the saints experienced more than their share of trials and temptations, and they grew as a result.

There is no group so holy, no place so far away, that it can shield us from all distractions and difficulties. No one living on earth is entirely free from temptation. The reason is that we are born with the source of temptation within us; we are trapped by our own evil desire.

We are fallen people living east of Eden. Therefore tribulation will never leave us, and one temptation will always follow on the heels of another.

Many people try to run away from temptations only to fall even harder. Trying to escape is not the solution. What makes us stronger than any of our enemies is patience and humility. If you only try to avoid temptations outwardly (rather than pluck them out by the roots), you will not get very far. Like weeds in a poorly cultivated garden, they will soon return worse than before.

Gradually, by patience and persistence, with God's help, you will win a victory that could never be yours through the violence of your own fretful efforts.

Seek counsel when you are tempted, and don't be hard on someone else who is tempted. Give him the same loving support you would want for yourself.

Two things increase temptation's hold on you: an indecisive mind and little confidence in God. As a ship without a rudder is driven this way and that by the tossing waves, so the careless and irresolute person is battered by temptations on every side.

Fire tests iron; temptation tests an honest person. Sometimes we don't know what we can do until temptation shows us what we are.

But don't play with fire! It is far easier to deal successfully with temptation in the beginning, when the flames are still controllable. The time to deal with the enemy is while he remains outside the door of your heart. Take him on as soon as you hear the first knock. As Ovid said, "Prevent the illness; medicine comes too late."

First a mere thought comes to mind;
then a strong imagination works on it.
Pleasure may come,
followed by a tendency to evil,
and suddenly, we are hooked.

Little by little the enemy takes over because we let him get his foot in the door. The longer we put off resisting, the weaker we become.

Some people are tempted most strongly at the beginning of their spiritual life, others near the end. Some are troubled all their lives. Still others receive only light temptation. Such things are decided by God and we can trust his wisdom.

Therefore, we must not despair when we are tempted. Instead, we must pray to God all the more sincerely, asking him to help. Saint Paul has assured us, "Every test that you have experienced is the kind that normally comes to people. But God keeps his promises, and he will not allow you to be tested beyond your power to remain firm; at the time you are put to the test, he will give you the strength to endure it, and so provide you with a way out" (1 Cor. 10:13, Good News Bible).

"Humble yourselves, therefore, under God's mighty hand" (1 Pet. 5:6) in all temptation and difficulty, for he will save and honor those who are humble in spirit. It is no great accomplishment to be devout and fervent when your life is running smoothly, but patient endurance in troubled times is strong confirmation of your growth in grace.

Some are spared great temptations, only to be trapped by little ones each day. Being weak in small things, they never receive the big assignments.

Passing Judgment

Take a good look at yourself; don't judge what others do. Your evaluation of someone else will often be mistaken, but you can be fruitfully honest with yourself.

Living with Imperfections in Others

Try to be patient with the defects and blemishes in others, because you also have many things about you that they must endure. If you can't make yourself what you want to be, how can you expect to remake somebody else?

We would like to see another person perfect, and yet we ignore our own faults. We would be pleased if others were severely corrected, but we are reluctant to accept similar treatment for ourselves. We want the law to apply to everybody but ourselves. It is clear that we don't measure our neighbors and ourselves by the same standard.

If everyone were perfect, there would be nothing in others for us to bear with for God's sake. But God has seen to it that we must "carry each other's burdens" (Gal. 6:2).

For no one is without fault,
no one is without burden,
no one is self-sufficient,
no one is wise enough on his own.

Therefore, we must support one another, comfort one another, help, teach, and caution one another.

Peace Does Not Come from Others

Friend, if you expect to find peace in the friendship of any person, you are likely to be disappointed. But if you are intimate with God, the disloyalty or death of a friend will not crush you. Base your love for your friend on God, for without him, friendship is weak and won't last. Love that is bonded together by God is pure and true.

Life in a Monastery

You must learn how to overcome many of your own desires if you want to live peacefully and in harmony with others. It is a great accomplishment to live in a religious community or be a part of a congregation, without complaining, and to stick with it faithfully until you die.

You must be willing to seem a fool for Christ's sake if you want to live a religious life.

Wearing special clothes and shaving your head contribute almost nothing to your spiritual life, but changing your behavior and controlling your emotions make you truly religious.

If you pursue anything other than God and the salvation of your soul, you will find trouble and sorrow.

You will not have peace unless you try to be the least subordinate to all.

You came here to serve, not to rule. Now it is your duty to endure difficulties tolerantly and to work, not to rest idly and waste time in small talk.

Here, we are tested as gold in the furnace. Here, no one can stand the test—unless he is willing with all his heart to be humble before God.

Compare Yourself with Early Christians

Consider the early Christians' shining example of faithfulness, and you will see how little we do. There is no comparison!

The saints and followers of Christ served the Lord in hunger and thirst, in cold and nakedness, in toil and weariness, in observances and fasts, in prayer and holy meditation, in persecution and disgrace.

All day long they labored, and at night they prayed continually. Even at work, they prayed silently.

Every hour they spent with God seemed short. They enjoyed this communion so much they sometimes forgot to eat.

They were strangers to the world, but they were God's close companions.

After you have seen such examples of faith, it will be difficult for you to fall asleep spiritually.

Essentials for Each Day

A Christian ought to be as virtuous inside as he appears outside to others. No, he should be *better* in his heart than on the surface. Because God sees every part of us, we should be reverent before him and live as pure as angels in his sight.

We should pray every day, saying, "Help me, O Lord God! These are my good intentions in your service. Let me begin this day to settle down to the serious business of living a pure life, for what I have done so far is nothing."

The firmer we stick to our purpose, the more we will advance. And if the one who tries the hardest frequently fails, what will become of the less enthusiastic? Remember that our best intentions do not depend upon us for fulfillment, but upon God. We are to rely on him for whatever we try to do. You may make your plans, but the Lord determines your steps (Prov. 16:9).

Even if we do the best we can, we will still fail many times. Yet we must always plan something definite, plot a course, especially as we battle our greatest personal weaknesses.

Determine a plan of action in the morning, and then evaluate yourself at night. How have you behaved today? What were your words, your deeds, your thoughts? It may be that you have offended God or your neighbor.

Never be completely at rest. Read, or write, or pray, or meditate, or do something good for the community.

Everyone cannot profit from the same kind of spiritual practices; one is better for you, and another is better for someone else. In the same way we must choose spiritual practices that suit the occasion. There are different ways for dealing with holidays and regular days, temptation and peace, sadness and happiness.

The point is that we should prepare ourselves for a good departure from this earth.

"It will be good for that servant," says the gospel writer, Luke, "whom the master finds doing so when he returns. I tell you the truth, he will put him in charge of all his possessions" (Luke 12:43-44).

Enjoy Being Alone and Quiet

Watch for good times to retreat into yourself. Frequently meditate on how good God is to you. Skip the tricky questions. Read things that will move your heart.

If you will stop chattering and gossiping, you will find plenty of time for valuable meditation.

You will find in your "closet of prayer" what you frequently lose when you are out in the world. The more you visit it, the more you will want to return. But the longer you avoid it, the harder it will be to come back. If you are faithful to your secret place, it will become your closest friend and bring you much comfort. In silence and stillness, a devout person grows spiritually and learns the hidden things of the Bible. The tears shed there bring cleansing. God will draw near the person who withdraws for a while.

It is better for you to look after yourself this way in private than to perform wonders in public while neglecting your soul.

Turn to God Almighty. Ask him to forgive your sins and oversights. Leave trivial things to the trivial. "Go into your room, close the door" (Matt. 6:6), and speak with Jesus, your Beloved. Stay there with him. Nowhere else will you find this kind of peace.

Dealing with Malicious Gossip

Friend, stay near God and don't worry about what others think of you when you have a clear conscience. It is a good thing to suffer such misjudgment. If you are humble, it won't even bother you. Many people say things that are not worth hearing.

It is impossible to satisfy everyone. Paul became "all things to all men" (1 Cor. 9:22). And yet he said, "I care very little if I am judged by you or by any human court; indeed, I do not even judge myself" (1 Cor. 4:3). He did everything he could to lead others to Christ, but he still had plenty of detractors. This is how Paul preserved his sanity: he turned it all over to God who knows everything. When necessary, Paul faced those who tried to raise their own status by climbing over him. He answered their charges with humility and patience in order to protect others who might be hurt by his silence.

"I, even I, am he who comforts you.
Who are you that you fear mortal men,
the sons of men, who are but grass?" (Isa. 51:12).

What power does anyone have to injure you with words? He hurts himself, not you. And he will be unable to escape God's judgment, regardless of who he is. Keep God in sight and ignore others' abuse.

Understanding Human Misery

You will suffer, wherever you are, unless you are with God.

Why are you upset when things don't go the way you wish? Who gets everything his way? I don't. You don't. No one does. Not one person on earth—not even a king or a pope—has a problem-free life. Do you know who can deal with troubles best? It is the person who is willing to suffer something for God.

Thoughtless people say, "Look at the happy life that person leads! Money! Prestige! Power!" But if you consider the riches of heaven, you will see that these earthly things are inconsequential, undependable, and more a burden than a privilege. They are always accompanied by anxiety and fear. Our happiness does not depend upon owning a lot of things; enough to get along will do.

Life on earth involves misery. The spiritually perceptive person is even more aware of this because he sees clearly the effects of human corruption.

For that matter, to eat and drink, to sleep and wake, to work and rest, and to be forced to obey the other requirements of nature can become a great annoyance to a devout person who would almost prefer to live without a body!

Friend, don't give up your spiritual journey. You still have time. Why do you keep putting off your decision day after day? You can start immediately. You can say, "This is the moment to start moving. Now is the time to begin the fight and to change my ways."

How great is our weakness of character! Today you will confess your sins; tomorrow you will commit the same ones again. Right now, you intend to do better. In an hour, you will behave as though this moment never happened.

We have every reason, therefore, to be humble—we are so weak and unstable.

Thinking about Death

You won't last long here. Think about what will become of you in another world. You are here today and gone tomorrow.

How sad is the dullness and hardness of our hearts! We only think about the present and have little concern for what is to come.

Instead, we should plan every word and action as though we were going to die today. If you had a clean conscience you would not be afraid to die. It is better to run away from sin than from death. If you are not ready for death today, do you think you will be any more prepared tomorrow? Tomorrow is not guaranteed. How can you be sure you'll even live until tomorrow?

Living a long time doesn't make us better persons automatically. Sometimes the years increase only our burden of guilt, not the quality of our behavior. It would be wonderful if we could live even one day well. Many can tell you the date of their conversion, but their lives have little to show for it.

The person who thinks about his own death and daily prepares to die will be blessed. If you ever watch another person die, remember that you must also pass the same way. When morning comes, think that you will not live until sunset. At night, don't promise yourself a morning. Always be ready. Live in such a way that death will never catch you unprepared. "You must always be ready, because the Son of Man will come at an hour when you do not expect him" (Matt. 24:44).

When your last hour comes, you will have a new perspective on your entire life, and you will be deeply troubled if you have been careless and negligent.

"I tell you, now is the time of God's favor, now is the day of salvation!" (2 Cor. 6:2). The time will come when you will beg for one day or one hour to make amends, and you may not be granted it.

Try to live now so that when your time comes to die, you will be glad rather than afraid. Discover how to die to the world so that you can start living with Christ.

It is foolish to think that you will have a long life. You can't even be sure you will get through today! Many have been snatched suddenly out of this world. Think of the times you have heard of someone drowning, or choking to death, or dying while playing a sport. Fire, weapons, sickness, violent thieves—these unexpected threats are constantly present with us. "[We] spring up like a flower and wither away; like a fleeting shadow, [we] do not endure" (Job 14:2).

Do it now. Do whatever you can do right now. You never know when your opportunity will be ended by death. While you have the time, start collecting heavenly treasures. Think about nothing but your spiritual health. Care about nothing but the things of God.

Live as a stranger and a refugee in this world—as one who has nothing to do with earthly things. Keep your heart free and lifted up to God, "For here we do not have an enduring city, but we are looking for the city that is to come" (Heb. 13:14). That is where to send your prayers, sighs, and tears. Then, when you die, your spirit will be joyfully at home with Christ.

Divine Judgment

Always consider the end—how you will stand before God, your judge, from whom nothing can be kept secret. He cannot be bribed, and will not be deceived by flimsy excuses, but will certainly judge you honestly. If you are sometimes disturbed by the expression on an angry person's face, how will you feel before God, who knows everything about your foolish and sinful life? The time to do your weeping and pleading is *now*, while it can still accomplish good for you and in you.

Here is a picture of a patient and purifying life:

Though you receive injuries, you are more troubled by the other's malice than by any wrong done to you. You willingly pray for your enemies, and sincerely forgive them. If you have offended or hurt someone else, you are quick to ask for pardon.
Compassion is stronger in you than anger.
You passionately overcome your own will in order to subdue your body to your spirit.

It is better to eliminate sinful behavior here than to deal with it hereafter. What fuel shall the fires have but your sins?

There is no future in anything, then, except loving and serving God. If you love God with all your heart, you will not be afraid of death, or punishment, or judgment, or hell. Perfect love brings divine security. But if that love is not yet strong enough in you to keep you from sinning, then maybe the fear of hell will restrain you.

Good Advice for Good Living

"Trust in the Lord and do good;
dwell in the land and enjoy safe pasture.
Delight in the Lord
and he will give you the desires of your heart.
Commit your way to the Lord;
trust in him, and he will do this" (Ps. 37:3-5).

Carefully avoid in yourself those things that disturb you in others.

Pick some profitable fruit wherever you are. If you see or hear a good example, burn the imitation of it into your soul. But if you observe behavior that is harmful, avoid it like a snake. And if you already have committed the same sin yourself, get busy and make amends. Just as you observe others' actions, they observe yours.

You will always be glad at night, if you have lived the day fruitfully. Cautiously watch yourself. Whatever happens to others, don't neglect your own spiritual life.

PART II

Advice Concerning Inward Things

The Inner Life

"The kingdom of God is within you," says the Lord (Luke 17:21). Turn wholeheartedly to God, give up this miserable world, and you will discover rest for your soul. Learn to scorn outward things; concentrate on what goes on inside yourself. If you do, you will see the Kingdom of God come to you. "The kingdom of God is not a matter of eating and drinking, but of righteousness, peace and joy in the Holy Spirit" (Rom. 14:17). And that is not given to vicious people. Christ will come to you, bringing his special consolation with him, if you prepare a worthy place for him within yourself. The glory and beauty of Christ is an inner thing. He enjoys frequent visits quietly inside you. His conversation is deliciously pleasant; his comfort and peace are tremendous. It is marvelous to be his familiar friend.

Prepare yourself, faithful soul, to welcome your lover, that he may come to you and live with you as your spouse. This is what he says, "Whoever has my commandments and obeys them, he is the one who loves me. He who loves me will be loved by my Father, and I too will love him and show myself to him" (John 14:21).

When you have Christ, you are rich. He is enough. He will provide everything you need so you won't have to count on others without him. People change and fail. You cannot depend on them. Those who are for you today may be against you tomorrow. They are as variable as the wind. But Christ is eternally faithful.

Put all of your trust in God. Reverently love him. He will look out for you. "For here we do not have an enduring city, but we are looking for the city that is to come" (Heb. 13:14). Wherever you may be, you are a stranger and a pilgrim. You will never really rest until you are united inwardly with Christ. Why are you looking around for a resting place here? This is not your home; heaven is. Everything here is transitory, and you are no exception.

If you need help in learning how to meditate on high and heavenly things, think about Christ's willingness to die on the cross. Live for a while in his sacred wounds. This will bring you great comfort in tribulation, and will take the sting out of any trouble the world sends your way. Christ was in the world just as you are. He was despised and rejected, and his best friends deserted him when he was in deep trouble.

Christ was willing to suffer; do you dare to complain? Christ had enemies and detractors; so you want everyone to be your friend and benefactor?

There is no way your patience can receive a heavenly crown if you face no earthly problems. If you will not accept any opposition, how will you be Christ's friend? If even once you have truly discovered the secrets of the Lord Jesus, and tasted a sample of his great love, then you will not care two cents for your own convenience or inconvenience.

A lover of Jesus and of the Truth, a genuinely sincere Christian who is free from encumbering desires can spontaneously turn to God, lift himself above himself spiritually, and fruitfully linger there.

If you can evaluate things as they really are, and not as people report them to be, then you are wise, and God is your teacher.

Humility

Don't pay much attention to who is for you and who is against you. This is your major concern: that God be with you in everything you do. If you have a good conscience, God will be your defender and no person can hurt you. If you suffer silently, you will see how the Lord can help. God knows when and how to rescue you. Trust him.

It can be helpful for others to know our faults and blame us for them. Such experiences keep us humble, and humility goes a long way toward reconciling us to others.

God protects and helps the humble; he loves and comforts them.
He notices their humility; he pours out his grace on them.
When a humble one has been cast down, God raises him to glory.
He tells his secrets to the humble.
He draws them by invitation to himself.

If you are humble, you will be at peace even while experiencing shame, because your foundation is God and not the world. Don't think that you have made any progress at all until you see less virtue in yourself than in anybody else.

It Is Good to Be Peaceable

If you are at peace yourself, then you will be able to help others become peaceable. An excitable person distorts things and readily believes the worst, but a calm person can turn even bad circumstances into good ones. If you are at peace, you will not be suspicious of others. But if you are discontented and troubled, you will be agitated with all kinds of suspicions. You will be unable to remain quiet yourself, and you will not let anyone else rest either.

Accuse yourself and excuse another. See how far you are from genuine love and humility, which do not know how to be angry or indignant toward anyone else. It is no significant accomplishment to live with good and gentle people. Everybody enjoys compatible company! But to be able to get along with obstinate, disorderly, and contrary people is a unique gift, a highly commendable feat.

The person who knows best how to suffer will enjoy the most peace. Such a person has conquered himself and has become a lord of the world, a friend of Christ, and an inheritor of heaven.

Simplicity and Purity

These two wings will lift you high above earthly things: simplicity and purity. Simplicity of intention is after God's own heart; purity of affection sees him and tastes him. If you intend to look for nothing but the will of God and the good of your neighbor, you will enjoy abundant inner freedom.

If your soul is healthy, then every creature you see will be a living mirror, a book of sacred doctrine. There is no creature, regardless of its apparent insignificance, that fails to show us something of God's goodness. If you were inwardly good and pure, you would be able to comprehend everything easily. An unblemished heart penetrates heaven and hell.

What you are inside will color your judgment. If there is joy in this world, it is the pure in heart who experience it. And if there is suffering and anguish anywhere, it is all too familiar to the bad conscience.

As iron put into a fire loses its rust and glows red in the heat, so the one who turns completely to God wakes up and becomes a new person. It is when you begin to cool that you start fearing any little demand made of you, and you seek escape in earthly ways. But when, with God's help, you begin to gain control of yourself, you will pay little attention to things that used to bother you deeply.

What Comes Naturally—and What Is a Gift from God

Don't be fooled by what only appears to be good. Human nature and grace move in opposite directions. Here is how to tell the difference between the two.

Human nature is tricky and often misleads and traps; it always cares about itself. But grace simply avoids guile and cares about God.

Human nature puts up a fight and dies reluctantly; it is not easily taught new patterns or held under control. Grace avoids sensuality, desires to be held in check, and will not abuse freedoms.

Human nature always works for its own profit and advantage and seeks all it can gain from others. Grace does not think at all about itself, but instead about what is good for others.

Human nature accepts flattery, honor, and adulation gladly. Grace passes on the honor and worship to God.

Human nature hates to be shamed or rejected, but grace is pleased to endure such things in the name of God and accepts them as special favors when they come.

Human nature desires exotic and exclusive things. But grace enjoys the ordinary, and is willing to be dressed in simple clothes.

Human nature is greedy and finds receiving more blessed than giving. It enjoys owning private property. But grace is generous to the poor and content with a little. It knows "it is more blessed to give than to receive" (Acts 20:35).

Human nature does nothing because of generosity. Its constant aim is to gain the advantage. It wants praise and notoriety. But grace looks for no rewards beyond God and cares nothing for empty applause.

Human nature desires to have many friends and relatives and takes pride in its pedigree. It enjoys being among rich and important people. But grace loves its enemies and places virtue above noble birth. It sympathizes more with the innocent than with the influential, and finds truth more impressive than propaganda.

Human nature wants recognition. It wants admiration for good deeds. But grace hides its good works and private devotion and gives all praise to God.

Such grace is a heavenly light, a gift from God. It is the mark of a truly spiritual person. As nature is restrained, grace increases, and the soul becomes stamped with the image of God.

How to Think of Yourself

Don't trust your own judgment about yourself. We usually lack the grace or understanding to see clearly. The little light that is in us is quickly lost because of our negligence. Our spiritual vision is poorer than we realize. We frequently do something wrong, and then make it worse with excuses. Sometimes we are motivated by uncontrollable emotion and consider it "righteous indignation." We direct attention to small flaws in others while disregarding far worse things in ourselves. We carefully count others' offenses against us, but we rarely consider what others may suffer because of us. If we look at ourselves honestly, we will judge others less harshly.

If you are a genuine Christian, you will look for your own faults first, and you will keep silent about others' shortcomings. If you are totally absorbed in your personal relationship with God, you won't meddle in other lives.

Where are you when you are not with yourself? And when you have been everywhere and examined everybody else, what good will it do if you have neglected yourself?

If you want peace and unity of purpose, then you must put everything else out of sight. You will fail miserably if you value anything material. Let nothing be important for you, nothing high, nothing pleasant, nothing acceptable, unless it is simply God, or something that pleases God. Think of creature comforts as a waste of energy. A soul that loves God is not satisfied with anything less than God. God alone is eternal, infinite, present everywhere. He alone can comfort the soul and make the heart glad.

The Joy of a Clean Conscience

The glory of a good person is the evidence of a clean conscience. Keep your conscience clear and you will be happy. A good conscience is able to bear a heavy load and it will encourage you when you are under attack. A bad conscience is always afraid and uneasy.

Your sleep will be sweet if your heart does not accuse you.

Scoundrels are never really happy. They have no peace. " 'There is no peace,' says the LORD, 'for the wicked' " (Isa. 48:22).

And if they say, "No harm will come to us," don't believe them. God's wrath will one day surprise them, and their works and ideas will perish.

The praise of the world is short-lived and always accompanied by sorrow. The glory of the good is in their consciences, not in the comments of others.

Anyone who goes looking for stardom and does not count fame unimportant reveals little fondness for heavenly things. The most tranquil person of all is the one who cares about neither the praise nor the fault-finding of others. You are not a better person because you are praised; neither are you any worse if somebody denigrates you. You are what you are. Words can't change that. God knows what you are. If you really get to know your inner self, you won't care what anyone says about you. People consider actions, but God evaluates intentions.

If you are not looking for stardom, you have clearly committed yourself to God, "For it is not the one who commends himself who is approved, but the one whom the Lord commends" (2 Cor. 10:18).

To be God's close friend, and not to be a slave to any earthly desire, is the mark of a spiritual person.

Loving Jesus Comes First

Happiness comes to the person who knows how to love Jesus and to disregard himself for Christ's sake. Our love for Jesus must exceed all other loves. Love the world and you will collapse when it collapses; embrace Jesus and you will have stability forever.

Love him. Keep him as a friend. When all others forsake you, he will remain faithful to the end.

Eventually whether you choose it or not, you will be separated from everyone else. Therefore, stay close to Jesus in both life and death. Trust his fidelity. When all others fail, he alone can help you.

It is your Beloved's nature to desire no rivals, to ask for your full devotion.

If you look for Jesus in all things, you will certainly find him. And if you look only for yourself, you will find only yourself, but it will be your loss. Those who do not seek Jesus bring more harm on themselves than all their enemies could ever inflict.

How to Be Christ's Close Friend

When Jesus is with us, all is well and nothing seems insurmountable. But when Jesus is absent, everything is difficult. If Jesus does not speak to us inwardly, all other comfort is meaningless. But the slightest communication from him brings consolation. Recall how Mary Magdalene immediately stopped crying when Martha said to her, "The Teacher is here, and is asking for you" (John 11:28). It is a delightful moment when Jesus calls us from tears to spiritual joy!

Life without Jesus is like a dry garden baking in the sun. It is foolish to want anything that conflicts with Jesus. What can the world give you without Jesus? His absence is hell; his presence, paradise. If Jesus is with you, no enemy can injure you. Whoever finds Jesus has discovered a great treasure, the best of all possible good. The loss of him is a tremendous misfortune, more than the loss of the entire world. Poverty is life without Jesus, but close friendship with him is incalculable wealth.

We must develop our skill as carefully as an artist does if we want to live intimately with Jesus. Be humble and peaceable, and Jesus will be with you. Be devout and quiet, and Jesus will reside with you.

You may drive him out of your life if you return to outward things. And if you should repel him, and lose him, where will you run to find a friend? Life is nothing without a friend, and if Jesus isn't your best friend you will be sad and lonely. It would be better to have the entire world against us rather than to offend Jesus.

Make many friends; love them dearly. But love Jesus in a special way. Love others because of Jesus, but love Jesus for himself. For him, and in him, love both your friends and your enemies. Pray for them all, asking God to lead them to know and love Jesus also. Never seek this kind of devoted love for yourself. Such devotion belongs to God alone.

If discouraging and unpleasant days come your way, don't be despondent or defeated. Stand strong in God and bear whatever you must to the glory of Jesus Christ. For after winter, summer comes; after night, the day returns; and after a storm, calm is restored.

When We Can Find No Comfort

It is not difficult to be independent of human comfort when we have God's comfort. It is a great thing, an *extremely* great thing, to be able to live without both human and divine comfort, to be willing to endure cheerfully an exile of the heart for the honor of God, to ask nothing for yourself, and to claim no special favors because of your good works.

Why should anyone be impressed if you are happy and faithful when everything is going your way? God's grace gives a smooth ride. It isn't surprising that you don't feel your burden if the Almighty is carrying it for you!

You must go through a long and tremendous conflict within yourself before you can begin to master yourself and give your heart to God.

Therefore, when God comforts you spiritually, receive it with gratitude. You can be sure it is his gift to you—you did not deserve it. Don't let that gift swell you with pride. Instead, accept it in humility. And watch your step! That moment of comfort will also pass, and new temptations await you around the next corner.

If you should temporarily lose your sense of well-being, don't be too quick to despair. With humility and patience, wait for God who is able to give you back even more profound comfort.

There is nothing novel about this to those who are familiar with God's ways. The great saints and ancient prophets frequently experienced the alternation of up and down, joy and sorrow. One of them, while he was enjoying a mountain-top experience said:

"When I felt secure, I said,
'I will never be shaken.'
O LORD, when you favored me,
you made my mountain stand firm;
but when you hid your face,
I was dismayed" (Ps. 30:6-7).

And yet, even while he was going through this time, he did not feel crushed. With renewed passion, he prayed:

"Hear, O LORD, and be merciful to me;
O LORD, be my help" (Ps. 30:10).

In time, his prayer was answered. This is his report:

"You turned my wailing into dancing;
you removed my sackcloth and
clothed me with joy" (Ps. 30:11).

If great saints are exposed to such variations, we who are poor and weak should not be discouraged if our spiritual life fails to be uniformly ecstatic. The Holy Spirit gives and takes according to his own divine purpose.

Where shall I place my hope and confidence except in God's great mercy? For whether I am in good company, or have with me faithful friends, or religious books, or beautiful writings, or sweet music, all of these are little help when God seems far from me and I am left alone in the poverty of my being.

I have never met anyone so religious and devout that he has not felt occasionally some withdrawing of grace, some decrease in his spiritual consciousness. No saint was ever so enraptured and inspired that he escaped temptation before and after the great moment. Anyone who has never suffered a little for God's sake is not worthy of deep spiritual contemplation.

Remember the promise of heavenly comfort: "To him who over-comes, I will give the right to eat from the tree of life, which is in the paradise of God" (Rev. 2:7).

The devil never sleeps, and your flesh is very much alive. There-fore, constantly prepare yourself for battle. Surrounding you are enemies that never rest.

Be Thankful for God's Grace

You were born to work; why are you looking for rest? Adjust yourself to patience rather than to comfort, and to bearing the Cross rather than to mirth.

It is good of God to comfort us with his love. But we do evil when we fail to return it all to God again with thanksgiving. Ingratitude can stop the flow of God's love in us.

I will refuse any sort of consolation that destroys my repentance, and I will shrink from anything that leads to pride. Not all that is high is holy; neither are all enjoyable things good. Not every desire is pure; neither is everything that we cherish pleasing to God.

If you are taught by the gift of grace, and instructed by the terrible loss of it, you will not dare to claim any goodness in yourself; rather, you will admit that you are poor and naked. Give God what is God's and take credit for what is your own. In other words, thank God for his kindness and blame yourself for your own sin and the punish-ment it brings.

Always take the lowest place, and the highest will be given to you, for high structures require a solid foundation. The greatest, in the judgment of God, are the least in their own opinion; the more worthy they are, the more humility will be seen in them. People who are filled with honesty and heavenly glory don't look for empty praise. Those who are grounded in God simply cannot be conceited. If they recognize God as the giver of every good thing they have ever received, they don't seek applause from each other. They desire more than anything else that God may be praised in them.

Be thankful, therefore, for the smallest gift; then you will be worthy to receive greater things. Accept the most insignificant present as though it were something of special value. If you consider the worth of the Giver, no gift will seem trivial or worthless. Nothing given by almighty God can be of small value. Yes, even if he sends pain or sorrow, we should thank him for it, because he is always thinking of our eternal good.

Only a Few Love the Cross

Jesus has many who love his heavenly kingdom, but few who bear his Cross. Many want consolation, but few desire adversity. Many are eager to share Jesus' table, but few will join him in fasting. Everyone would be glad to rejoice with him, but not many are willing to suffer for him. Many will follow Jesus as far as the breaking of bread, but few will stay to drink the cup of his passionate self-sacrifice. Many are inspired by his miracles, but few accept the shame of his Cross. Many love Jesus as long as they have no troubles. Many praise and bless him as long as they receive some comfort from him. But if Jesus hides himself, leaving them even briefly, they start complaining and become dejected.

But those who love Jesus for Jesus' sake, and not for any special privileges, bless him in all difficulties and anguish, as well as in times of great comfort. Even if he should never comfort them again, they would continue to praise and thank him. What astonishing power rests in the pure love of Jesus that is not corrupted with self-interest or self-love! One term describes those who are always looking for comfort: *mercenary*. Don't they show themselves to be lovers of self rather than Christ? All they care about is their own advantage and profit.

Where can we find anyone who is willing to serve God for nothing? It is rare to discover someone so spiritual! Do you know anyone who is truly poor in spirit and free from dependence on any created thing? Such a person "is worth far more than rubies!" (Prov. 31:10).

"If one were to give all the wealth of his house for love, it would be utterly scorned" (Song of Songs 8:7). And if someone tries hard to make amends for all of his sins, he still hasn't done very much. And if he receives the best education, he still has a long way to go. And if he is exceedingly virtuous and glowing with devotion, an essential ingredient is still lacking. What must he do? He must give up everything, especially himself, retaining no trace of selfishness. And when he has done everything required of him, he must consider it as nothing. He must not agree with others when they applaud him, but rather admit that he is actually an ordinary servant.

As the Gospel says, "When you have done everything you were told to do, say, 'We are unworthy servants; we have only done our duty' " (Luke 17:10). After admitting this he may be honestly poor in spirit, and may say with the psalmist, "Turn to me and be gracious to me, for I am lonely and afflicted" (Ps. 25:16).

And yet, no one will be richer, no one more powerful, no one more free, because he is able to leave himself and all material things behind, and set himself in the lowest place.

The Royal Highway of the Holy Cross

Many have difficulty with these words: "If anyone would come after me, he must deny himself and take up his cross and follow me" (Matt. 16:24). But they will find it even harder to hear that last statement: "Depart from me, you who are cursed, into the eternal fire . . ." (Matt. 25:41).

Those who gladly hear and follow Christ shall have no reason to fear such a condemnation. Every servant of the Cross who has lived like the crucified Christ will face the heavenly Judge with confidence. Why, then, are you afraid to carry your cross when it leads you to such a kingdom?

In the Cross is salvation,
in the Cross is life,
in the Cross is protection from our enemies,
in the Cross is good mental health,
in the Cross is spiritual joy,
in the Cross is virtue at its best,
in the Cross is the full perfection of holiness.

There is no salvation of soul, nor hope of eternal life, except in the Cross. Carry your cross and follow Jesus. He went first, carrying his cross, and then dying on it for you. If you are dead with him, you will also live with him. And if you share his punishment, you will also share his glory. Look far and wide and still you will not find a better way above, or a safer way below, than the highway of the holy Cross.

Even if you use the best judgment and make the best plans, you will still find it necessary to suffer, willingly or unwillingly. There is no escaping the Cross. You will feel either pain in your body or tribulation in your spirit. Sometimes you will feel deserted by God. Sometimes your neighbor will trouble you. Quite frankly, you will sometimes be a burden to yourself. As long as God wants you to bear it, there can be no remedy for your suffering, because there are some vital lessons you need to learn. You must subject yourself entirely to God, and become more humble by the things you suffer. No one is better able to appreciate the Passion of Christ than the one who has suffered similarly.

The Cross, therefore, is inescapable. It waits for you everywhere. No matter how far you run, you cannot hide from it. For wherever you go, you take yourself along. Above and below, inside and outside, everywhere you turn, you shall find the Cross.

If you carry the Cross willingly, it will carry you. It will lead you to the place where suffering comes to an end, a place we will not find here. If you are forced against your will to carry the cross, then you make it difficult for yourself, adding to your load. No matter what attitude you have, you must bear the burden. If you manage to throw away one cross, you will certainly find another, and it may be even heavier.

Do you think you can escape what no one else can avoid? Which of the saints was exempt? Not even our Lord Jesus Christ was spared! "Did not the Christ have to suffer these things and then enter his glory?" (Luke 24:26). How can you think you will find a way other than this royal highway of the holy Cross?

The whole life of Christ was a Cross and a martyrdom; do you want ease and recreation for yourself? You are making a grave mistake, and deceiving yourself, if you seek anything other than hardship. This mortal life is full of misery and it is marked on every side with crosses. The higher you advance in the Spirit, the heavier the crosses become, for the pain of exile increases in proportion to your love for God. And yet, a person afflicted in many ways still receives refreshing comfort if he sees the value of enduring crosses.

We are not naturally inclined

to bear the Cross,
to love the Cross,
to discipline our bodies,
to run away from honors,
to suffer reproach willingly,
to disregard ourselves and to wish to be disregarded,
to endure all trouble and loss,
to desire no prosperity in this world.

If you try to accomplish these things yourself, you will fail. But if you trust the Lord, you will receive divine strength, and you will be able to withstand the world and control your flesh.

Decide, then, like Christ's good and faithful servant, to bear courageously the Cross of your Lord, who, because of his love for you, was crucified. Drink heartily of the Lord's cup if you want to be his friend. As for comfort, leave that to God; let him do what he will. Accept suffering graciously. "I consider that our present sufferings are not worth comparing with the glory that will be revealed in us" (Rom. 8:18).

When you have reached such a point, all misery will seem sweet and you will relish it for Christ's sake and think that you have discovered paradise on earth.

As long as you object to suffering you will be ill at ease. Accept it, and you will find peace.

Even if you were caught up in the ecstasy of the third heaven with Paul, you would still face adversity. "I [says Christ] will show him how much he must suffer for my name" (Acts 9:16). Therefore, you must suffer if you desire to love Jesus and to serve him always. If only you were worthy to suffer something for the name of Jesus! How much glory would be yours; what joy all God's saints would feel; how much you would teach your neighbor! For everyone advises patience, but few are willing to suffer.

Without doubt, you ought to lead a dying life. The more you die to yourself here, the more you begin to live for God. You are unprepared to comprehend heavenly things until you can submit to adversities for Christ's sake. Nothing is more acceptable to God, nothing more wholesome for you, than to suffer cheerfully for Christ. And if you have a choice, take the hard road. This will make you more like Christ.

You can be sure that if there had been a better way to man's salvation than suffering, Christ would have followed it. He plainly taught the bearing of the Cross. "If anyone would come after me, he must deny himself and take up his cross daily and follow me" (Luke 9:23).

When we have read and searched through everything, this will be our ultimate conclusion: "We must go through many hardships to enter the kingdom of God" (Acts 14:22).

PART III

Conversations with God

Christ Speaks Inwardly to the Faithful Soul

I will listen to what the Lord God says in me. That soul is blessed who hears the Lord speaking and inwardly receives his words of comfort.

Blessed are the ears that hear the divine whisper and ignore the murmuring of the world.

Truly blessed are the ears that listen to no external voice, but to the truth that is taught within.

Blessed are the eyes that are closed, focusing inwardly on eternal things.

Blessed are the ones who can enter deeply within themselves; who prepare themselves more and more, by daily exercises, to receive heavenly secrets.

Blessed are those who take time for God, who shake off all the encumbering cares of the world.

Think about these things, O my soul, and close the door on your physical senses, that you may hear what God says within you.

Thus says your Beloved: "I am your salvation, your peace, your life. Stay with me, and you shall find peace. Release everything that is transitory. Let it pass away. Look for the lasting things. Short-term pleasures are seductive, but they will disappoint you. What good is everything in all creation to you if you are not in close fellowship with the Creator? Therefore, get rid of all earthly things.

"Try to please your Maker. Be faithful to me. That way you'll discover true happiness."

The Truth Speaks within Us without Noisy Words

Speak, Lord, your servant is listening. I am your servant; help me to know and understand what you are saying. Let your teaching distill like dew.

Long ago, the Hebrews said to Moses, "Speak to us yourself and we will listen. But do not have God speak to us or we will die" (Exod. 20:19).

But Lord, that is not what I pray. Instead, in all humility, I earnestly say with Samuel, "Speak, Lord, your servant is listening."

I am not listening now to Moses or any other prophet. I am listening for *you*, O God, the one who inspired and enlightened all the prophets. You alone can instruct me perfectly, and they can teach me nothing without you.

The prophets may speak words, but they cannot give the Spirit.

Their language is beautiful, but if you are silent, it will not set my heart on fire.

They give the words, but you give the words meaning.

They present mysteries, but you unlock what is hidden.

They announce commandments, but you help me keep them.

They show the way, but you give me strength to walk in it.

They reach my outward senses, but you enlighten me inwardly.

They water the garden, but you make the plants grow.

They cry out with words, but you help me understand.

Therefore, O Lord, speak your eternal truth to me through their words, so my life will not remain unfruitful. Then you will not condemn me for having heard without responding, for having known without loving, for having believed without obeying.

Speak, Lord, your servant is listening. You have the words of eternal life. Speak to me. Comfort my soul. Transform my life. I will give praise, glory, and honor to you always.

God Is to Be Heard with Humility

Hear my words, my child—wholesome words that surpass all the knowledge of the philosophers and sages. My words are spirit and life and can never be compared with the wisdom of the world. They are not to be misused for self-satisfaction, but to be heard in silence, and received with humility and great affection.

"Blessed is the man you discipline, O LORD,
the man you teach from your law;
you grant him relief from days of trouble" (Ps. 94:12-13).

I am the one who taught the prophets from the beginning. Even now I continue to speak to everyone, but many are spiritually deaf and do not hear my voice. Most people listen more eagerly to the world than to me. The world promises fleeting things of little value and people strive for them. I offer things of highest quality that endure forever, and people yawn in apathy.

Is there anyone who serves me with the same care and devotion given to the world and its leaders? To gain a few dollars, a long trip may be taken; for eternal life, many will barely lift a foot from the ground.

Blush with shame! You do not care at all for permanent good, for the reward beyond all price, for the highest honor and glory that will last forever. Be ashamed, you lazy and complaining servant! You are more anxious to work for death than for life.

Those who seek earthly rewards will be disappointed frequently, but my promises deceive no one. I will not send anyone away empty if he trusts me. I will give what I promise. I will do what I say. I only require that a person remain faithful in my love.

Write my words in your heart; diligently meditate upon them. You will see how important they are to you when you are tempted. Even if you can't understand the meaning now, keep reading. A time will come when you will need those words and then you will understand.

I visit my friends in two ways:

1. with trials and temptations;
2. with consolation.

And I teach two lessons as the days go by:

1. Get rid of your vices.
2. Increase your virtues.

"Whoever rejects me and does not accept my message has one who will judge him. The words I have spoken will be his judge on the last day!" (John 12:48).

A Prayer for the Grace of Devotion

O Lord, my God! You are everything that is good. Who am I, that I should dare to speak to you? I am your poorest, least deserving servant—lowlier than I would like to admit.

Yet remember me, O Lord, because
  I am nothing,
  and I can do nothing.
Only you are good, just, and holy.
  You can do all things.
  You can supply all things.
  You fill all things,
leaving empty only the person who lives apart from you.

In your mercy, fill my heart with grace. How can I endure this life without your strength and mercy?

"Do not hide your face from your servant;
answer me quickly, for I am in trouble.
Come near and rescue me;
redeem me because of my foes" (Ps. 69:17-18).

"I spread out my hands to you;
my soul thirsts for you like a parched land.
Teach me to do your will,
for you are my God;
may your good spirit lead me on level ground" (Ps. 143:6, 10).

Teach me to do your will, O Lord, teach me to live worthily and humbly before you; for you are my wisdom, you know me intimately; you knew me before the world was made, and before I was born in the world.

Our Honest Humility
Before God

My child, live honestly before me, and always look for me with a simple heart. This will defend you from evil and set you free from deceivers and unjust slanderers. If the truth sets you free, then you will be really free, and you will pay no attention to the empty comments of others.

That's true, Lord. Let it be for me as you say. I want your Truth to teach me, guard me, and preserve me until the end of my days. Let it free me from every evil, and I will walk with you in liberty.

The Truth speaks: I will teach you what is pleasing to me. Think about your sins with great displeasure and sadness. Never think highly of yourself because you have done some good things.

The fact is, you are a sinner. Many passions entangle and enslave you. By yourself you will always be quickly defeated, quickly overcome, quickly disturbed, quickly unnerved.

You have nothing to be proud of, and much that should shame you. You are far weaker than you can comprehend.

Therefore, do not let anything you do seem very important to you. Let nothing seem great, nothing precious or admirable, nothing sophisticated, nothing high, nothing really worth having, except that which is eternal.

Take pleasure, above all else, in the eternal Truth. Always be displeased with your own unworthiness. The thing to fear, the thing to blame and run away from, is your sin, which ought to bother you more than the loss of any material thing.

Some are not sincere. Curiosity and pride make them wish to know my secrets and understand God's profundity. All the while they neglect themselves and their own salvation.

Some have their devotion only in books, some in paintings, some in statues and carvings.

Some have me often enough on their lips, but they have little of me in their hearts.

Others, with insight and self-denial, seek the eternal at all times. They are reluctant to hear about earthly things and are upset by the demands of nature. These understand what the Spirit of Truth says to them: disregard the world, and long for heaven.

The Results of Divine Love

I bless you, heavenly Father, Father of my Lord Jesus Christ, because you take notice of a creature like me. Merciful Father and God of all comfort, I give you thanks.

Come then, Lord God, Holy One who loves me! When you come into my heart, everything in me will leap with joy!

"You are my hiding place;
you will protect me from trouble
and surround me with songs of deliverance" (Ps. 32:7).

Because I am still imperfect and weak in love, I need your strength and comfort. Visit me frequently and teach me with holy discipline.

Free me from evil passions, and heal my heart of excessive desires; that being inwardly healthy, I may be prepared to love, and filled with courage to endure and persevere.

Love is a great good that makes every heavy thing light. It is not burdened by the load it carries, and it sweetens the bitter. Jesus' noble love inspires us to do great things and to long for a more nearly perfect life. Love wants to live in the heights, and not to be grounded by base things.

Nothing is sweeter than love,
nothing stronger,
nothing wider,
nothing more pleasant,
nothing more satisfying in heaven or on earth.

Because you, my God, give birth to love, you are love's natural resting place.

The one in love rejoices in his freedom. He gives all for everything, because he is familiar with One who is supreme above all—the Source of all that is good. He concentrates not on the gifts, but on the Giver.

Love does not meet standard requirements; it goes beyond all measurements.

Love notices no burdens,
thinks nothing of its labors,
willingly does more than it is able,
pleads no excuse of impossibility;
believes it can accomplish anything.

And it can. It makes up for many shortcomings; it opens the door for many possibilities.

Anyone in love knows what I am talking about.

Enlarge your love in me, Lord. I desire to swim in a sea of your love. I want to be possessed by love so that I can rise above myself. Let me sing love's song. Let me follow you, my Beloved. Let me love you more than myself, and love myself only for you.

Love treads lightly. It is sincere, kind, pleasant, and delightful. It is strong, patient, faithful, careful, longsuffering, brave, and never selfish.

Toward you, Lord, love must be devout and thankful—trusting and hoping always, even when I do not taste your sweetness. For no one can live in love without some pain.

If I am not ready to suffer all things, and to accept your will, I am not worthy of the title *lover.*

A lover is willing to embrace the difficult and the bitter, for the sake of his Beloved.

How to Recognize a True Lover

Child, you are not yet a true lover.

Why, O Lord?

Because you give up when a little opposition comes your way. You are too eager for consolation. A genuine lover stands his ground when tempted. He does not yield to the Enemy. "I am not saying this because I am in need, for I have learned to be content whatever the circumstances" (Phil. 4:11).

A true lover looks less at the gift and more at the love of the giver. He regards the demonstration of affection as more important than the value of the gift, and prizes the one loved more than any present.

Therefore, all is not lost if you sometimes feel less devotion toward me than you would like. Even the affection you sometimes have is one of my gifts to you—something of a foretaste of heaven. Don't count on it too much, because it comes and goes. But do resist the tendency of your mind toward evil, and reject the suggestions of the devil.

Be strong! It is not an illusion that sometimes you are ecstatically carried away and then you return to your familiar faults. It seems that you unwillingly tolerate this shift, and as long as it is unpleasant to you, and you resist it, you will be rewarded.

Remember that your old Enemy tries with every trick he has to frustrate your desire for good and to divert your attention from worship. He suggests many evil thoughts, hoping to fatigue you and frighten you away from prayer and holy reading. He hates humble confession; if he could manage it, he would even talk you out of Holy Communion.

Don't listen to him! Ignore his deceitful traps. When he recommends anything evil, say to him:

"Get behind me, Satan! You are a stumbling block to me; you do not have in mind the things of God, but the things of man" (Matt. 16:23).

"The Lord is my light and my salvation—
whom shall I fear?
The LORD is the stronghold of my life—
of whom shall I be afraid?" (Ps. 27:1).

"Though an army besiege me,
my heart will not fear;
though war break out against me,
even then will I be confident" (Ps. 27:3).

Fight like a good soldier. And if, because you are weak, you sometimes fall, get up again strengthened by the experience, trusting my abundant grace. Then guard yourself against complacency and pride. Be warned by the fall of the proud who rely upon their own strength. Always be humble.

The Privacy of Devotion

My child, it is best for you to be private with your devotion. Don't think highly of yourself or talk too much about it. Don't let the quality of your devotion be an obsession. It is better to think less of yourself and to consider yourself unworthy of this grace.

Some incautious people ruin themselves by attempting to produce an ecstatic devotional experience by their own will. Because they neglect to consider their own weakness, they attempt more than is pleasing to me and quickly lose all. Those who try to build a safe nest for themselves in heaven become helpless and thereby learn not to fly with their own wings, but to trust mine.

Those who think they are intelligent seldom accept guidance. It is better to have a little good judgment with humility, than great knowledge about many things with self-conceit. It is better for you to have little than much of what may make you proud.

You are not wise, if, in a moment of difficulty, you become despondent and lose your confidence in me. Those who are too secure in peacetime will be overly dejected in time of war.

When spiritual fervor has been ignited in you, meditate on how it will be when that light leaves you. And when this happens, remember that the light may return again and its loss may be profitable by my design.

Your value is not calculated by the number of visions you have, by your skill in the Scriptures, or by your position in relation to others.

You are most worthy if you are truly humble and full of divine love, and if you seek only My honor.

Standing in God's Presence

I will speak to you, Lord, even though I am nothing but dust and ashes.

If I begin to think highly of myself, you stand next to me, and my sins are obvious. I cannot deny them.

But if I am humble, and control my ego, and stop being self-centered, and reduce myself to the dust that surely I am, your grace will be gentle with me, and your light will come into my heart. Then all my self-esteem, however small it might be, will vanish in the deep valley of my nothingness.

In that place you will hold a mirror before me and show me what I am, what I have been, and what I have become; for I am nothing, and I did not know it.

See what happens when I am left to myself! I am nothing but weakness. But the very instant you show me your love, I become strong and filled with new joy. How wonderful to be suddenly free from my own heavy weight. Instead of sinking downward I am lifted up into your embrace!

Your love guards me from danger and assists me in so many ways. It preserves me from innumerable evils.

It is true, "The man who loves his life will lose it, while the man who hates his life in this world will keep it for eternal life" (John 12:25). By loving myself, I lose myself. But by looking only for you, and loving only you, I find both myself and you.

Blessed are you, my God. Even though I am unworthy, your generosity and goodness never cease. "He causes his sun to rise on the evil and the good, and sends rain on the righteous and the unrighteous" (Matt. 5:45).

Turn us in your direction, that we may be grateful, humble, and devout. You are our salvation, our courage, and our strength.

Putting God First

My child, I must be your life's supreme goal if you want genuine happiness. This will purify your intentions and keep you from perverse interest in yourself and earthly things. For if you put yourself first, you will begin to dry up and wither inside.

Give me first place, for I have given all. Think about how everything flows from the Greatest Good. I am the source, like a spring that produces a river. From my resources the small and the great, the poor and the rich, fill themselves, as from an inexhaustible fountain, with the water of life.

Those who willingly and freely serve me shall receive "one blessing after another" (John 1:16). But those who attempt to delight in anything other than me, or to enjoy some private pleasure, will not have true joy and will get into innumerable difficulties.

Therefore, don't take credit for anything good yourself, and don't attribute goodness to any other person. Give me the praise; for without me no one amounts to anything.

I have given you everything you have and I want you to be grateful. This will check pride. And if you are filled with heavenly grace and genuine love, you will not be envious or narrowminded, and selfishness will be impossible for you. For divine love is stronger than all else and it enlarges the capacity of the soul.

If you are thinking clearly, you will rejoice in me alone and place all of your hope in me, for "there is only One who is good" (Matt. 19:17). I am to be praised above all things.

Serving God at Any Cost

Now I will speak again, O Lord. I will express myself in the presence of my Lord and my heavenly King.

"How great is your goodness,
which you have stored up for those who fear you,
which you bestow in the sight of men
on those who take refuge in you" (Ps. 31:19).

What difference do you make to those who love you and serve you with enthusiasm? You allow them the indescribable joy of contemplating you.

You have given me a special insight into the sweetness of your love: you gave me my life; when I wandered far away, you brought me back again to serve you; you wanted me to love you.

You are a waterfall of unceasing love! What shall I say about you? How can I forget you? You thought of me even when I was lost and desperate. You have been merciful beyond my wildest dream. You have been good to me far above anything I deserve.

How shall I pay you back? Most of us are not expected to give up everything, to renounce the world and begin a life of monastic solitude. Does it mean very much that I should serve you when all of creation exists for that purpose? I don't think so. But I see this, and it staggers me: you are willing to accept the service of someone as poor and unworthy as I. You will make me one of your beloved servants.

I am your servant! Everything I have is yours. But even as I say that, I know you are serving me more than I am serving you. At your command all of the resources of heaven and earth are at my disposal, and even the angels help me. Yet you serve me in a way that surpasses all of this: you promise to give yourself to me. You are the great Servant of us all.

With what gift can I return your favors? I want to serve you all the days of my life. I wish it were possible, just for one day, to do something worthwhile for you. You are my Lord, and I am a poor servant who is obligated to serve you with all my strength. I should never tire of praising you, for this is what I want to do. This is my desire. Compensate for what I lack.

Examine and Control Your Desires

My child, there are still many things you need to learn.

What are they, Lord?

That you desire only what will please me, and that you stop putting yourself first and earnestly seek my will.

Sometimes you are driven to distraction by desires that burn inside you. But try to determine whether your underlying motive is to honor me or simply to serve your own best interests. If you seek to honor me, you will find contentment whatever happens, but if selfishness hides within you, it will become your greatest burden.

Be careful, therefore, not to give in too easily to any desire without seeking my counsel.

Sometimes apparently good things are not desirable, and what is offensive at first sight often turns out to be the better choice.

It can be worthwhile to restrain even the best desires and inclinations. Excessive eagerness distracts the mind, a lack of discipline can lead to scandal, and, if others resist your wishes, the disappointment may turn you away from me.

Your sensual appetite may require extreme measures to control. It is not easy to disregard what your flesh likes and dislikes, and to train an unwilling body to be subject to the Spirit. You must work at this, and, eventually, your body will obey you. You will learn to be content with little, to be pleased with simple things, and not to complain about inconveniences.

Patience Wins Over Sensual Desires

O Lord, my God, I know that patience is necessary for me because many things disturb me every day. No matter what plans I make to keep myself at peace, I cannot avoid life's struggle and sorrow.

That is true, my child. I do not desire for you to enjoy an absolute peace, free from all temptations and hindrances. Instead, I want you to have peace even when you are troubled by unpleasant experiences.

Do you believe that prosperous people have an easy life? Ask them and you will find out otherwise. You may think they are carefree, and do not bleed like other people. But, even if all that nonsense is true at this moment, how long do you think it will last? "As smoke is blown away by the wind, may you blow them away" (Ps. 68:2). The time always comes when former pleasures can barely be recalled. These "privileged" people live with constant bitterness, weariness, and fear. The very things they enjoy so much often bring them sorrow. Such brief pleasures are false pleasures, but few can see this. Many forfeit their souls for small enjoyments in this corruptible life.

Therefore, "Don't be controlled by your lust; keep your passions in check" (Sirach 18:30). "Delight yourself in the LORD and he will give you the desires of your heart" (Ps. 37:4).

For you will only truly enjoy your life and receive my full comfort if you stop those practices that debase you. The less you depend upon earthly comfort, the sweeter you will find my consolation.

You will have some sadness when you begin this battle in yourself. Old habits will resist you, but you will win if you replace them with better habits. Your body will protest, but your spirit can gain the upper hand. The old serpent will tempt and harass you, but prayer will make him run away. And the best way to keep him away is to get busy with something constructive.

Following Christ's Example of Humble Obedience

My child, if you try to escape obedient service, you will miss my gift. A community has benefits that are unknown to the hermit.

If you are unable to submit freely and cheerfully to a superior, it is a sign that you do not have yourself under control. Learn how to submit quickly to a leader if you want to rule yourself. It is easier to defeat the outward enemy if the inward man is strong and controlled. The most troublesome enemy you have is yourself, if you are not in harmony with my Spirit.

It is an indication that you still love yourself too much if you are afraid to submit to others. What a paltry comparison if you, nothing but dust and ashes, submit yourself to others in the Lord, when I, the Almighty and most high God, the Creator of everything, subjected myself to the world for your sake! I became the most humble and submissive of all people, that you might overcome your pride with my humility.* Discover how to break your own wishes and give in to the will of others. Be firm with yourself and don't let pride swell your chest. Find out what it is like to let someone walk over you if necessary.

What do you have to complain about? If you were to receive what you have earned, you would be condemned to hell. But I have spared you because you are precious to me. I want you to know my love.

---

*The original author passed up a splendid opportunity to quote the great passage recorded in Philippians 2:6-11.

"He always had the nature of God,

but he did not think that by force he should try

to become equal with God.

Instead of this, of his own free will he gave up all he had,

and took the nature of a servant.

He became like man

and appeared in human likeness.

He was humble and walked the path of obedience

all the way to death—his death on the cross."

God Is Not Misled by a Few Good Deeds

Lord, I tremble before your thundering judgment. It astonishes me when I read:

"What is man, that he could be pure,

or one born of a woman, that he could be righteous?

If God places no trust in his holy ones,

if even the heavens are not pure in his eyes,
how much less man, who is vile and corrupt" (Job 15:14-16).

If angels are faulty, what can I say for myself? If stars even fall
from heaven, what can I expect? I have seen good and great people
stumble, and those who have eaten sacred bread now root with pigs.

The only good thing about me is what you give. The only clear
thoughts I have are a gift from you. I have no strength unless you
uphold me, no morality unless you protect me. Leave me on my
own, and I sink into death; guide me, and I am raised up to life.

How could I ever boast? Your judgment destroys my self-
righteousness. No one in the whole world can sit at the head table
when he has faced the Truth.

How to Pray for the Things We Want

My child, this is the way to pray: "Lord, if it is pleasing to you,
fulfill my request. If it is good for me, grant that I may use it for your
honor. But if you know that it will hurt me, take the desire away
from me."

Why pray like that? Because not every desire is inspired by the
Holy Spirit, even though it may seem right and good. Sometimes it
is hard to tell whether a notion is an inspiration or a temptation.
Many have been deceived.

Therefore, every request must be made with humility. You must
submit the entire matter to me, take yourself entirely out of it, and
say: "O Lord, you know what is best. Let this or that be done as you
please. Give what you choose, how much you choose, and when
you choose. Place me where you think best and treat me as you see
fit. I am in your hands. Turn me in one direction and then another;
I am your servant, prepared for anything. I have no desire to live for
myself, but only for you. How I wish I could do this perfectly!"

Trusting God

Friend, *let me do what is best for you. You see everything from a human point of view.*

Lord, you are right. You care about me more than I care about myself. Unless I trust you, I have no ground to stand upon. Do with me whatever you choose, because it can only be good. If you want me to be in darkness, I will bless you; if you want me to be in light, I will bless you again. If I am comforted, I will be grateful; and if I am afflicted I will be equally grateful.

My child, that is the way to think if you want to walk with me. Be as ready to suffer as to rejoice. Be as cheerful when poor as you would be when rich.

O Lord, for your sake I will gladly bear what I must, whatever it may be. I will accept good and evil, sweet and bitter, joy and sorrow, and for all of it I will give you thanks. As long as you stay close to me and never remove my name from the "book of life" (Rev. 3:5), whatever trouble I experience will not hurt me.

How to Take Slights and Injuries

My child, I gave up the glories of heaven and accepted the miseries of this world because of my love for you, intending that you might learn a little patience. From the moment of my birth until my death on the Cross, I experienced grief. I was deprived of many things. I heard many complaints against me. I calmly endured disgrace and taunting. For kindness I was repaid ingratitude. For miracles I received curses. When I spoke the truth, people argued with me.

My Lord, since you were patient, I also should bear myself patiently. Although life can be bleak, it can become bright again with your help. If you had not lived before us to show the way, how could we follow? Even now we are only halfhearted. What would become of us if we did not have such great light?

Genuine Patience

What are you saying, my child? Stop complaining! Think about my sacrifice and the suffering of other saints. "In your struggle against sin, you have not yet resisted to the point of shedding your blood" (Heb. 12:4).

You have suffered very little in comparison with others. Think about the heavy burdens others carry, and you will easily bear your own small troubles. And if you do not think yours are small, perhaps it is only because you are impatient. Whether they are small or great, try to bear your burdens without complaint.

Do not say, "I can't take it! I'm not required to take it! This person has hurt me deeply and accused me of things that are not true." That is foolish. It fails to take the crowning virtue of patience into account; it focuses on the offending person and the injury.

You are not patient if you are willing to accept difficulty only up to a certain point and from a few selected people. Genuine patience cares nothing about the source of the problem, whether it is from a superior, an equal, or an inferior, whether it is from a good and holy person or a villain. You must take it all thankfully, as though I gave it. Consider it your gain. For it is impossible that anything, however small, can be suffered for my sake without some reward.

Be ready for battle if you want to win. Without struggling you cannot gain patience, and if you will not suffer, you refuse to be crowned. Rest only follows labor.

Lord, let this become possible for me, even though it seems out of reach. You know I can endure so very little, and I am quickly defeated. Please let every difficulty become a desirable thing, for to suffer and to be harassed for you is beneficial to my soul.

Admitting Our Weakness

I will confess my weakness to you, O Lord. Sometimes when I intend to be courageous, I succumb even to a little temptation.

You know how frail I am, Lord. Have mercy on me. Do not let me get stuck in a quagmire of sin. I fall so easily. My passions are stronger than my will, and, although I am reluctant, they keep on nagging me. It is fatiguing to live every day in that kind of tension. I know I am weak, because temptations come to me far more easily than they depart.

What a strange life! Trouble and misery are always in stock. Traps and enemies are abundant. When one problem retreats, another takes its place. And sometimes the second difficulty doesn't wait for the first to be resolved.

How can anyone love a life like that? Isn't it natural to feel bitterness in the face of so much misery? Is anything so threatened by death and plague even worthy of the name, "life"? And yet people love it and try to find happiness in it. Some things make us love this world; other things make us hate it.

Complete Devotion to God

Above all else, and in everything, my soul must rest in God. Let me, O living Jesus, rest in you above every created thing,

above health and beauty,
above glory and honor,
above power and dignity,
above wisdom and cunning,
above riches and arts,
above joy and gladness,
above fame and praise,
above pleasure and comfort,
above hope and promise,
above things earned and things desired,
above gifts and favors,
above mirth and merrymaking.

Ultimately let me rest above angels and archangels and all the host of heaven, above things seen and unseen, above all that is not you, my God.

Because you, O Lord, are above all. You alone are most high,
most powerful,
most sufficient,
most full,
most pleasant,
most comforting.

No matter what gifts you give me, and regardless of your great self-revelation, if I do not know you as my closest friend, I am still hungry for you. I will never be content until my heart is devoted above all else to you.*

When will all this happen? When will I love you so much, my God, that I forget myself and know you alone?

Now, I sigh unhappily. I am hurt and grieved by the evil I see. I am hindered and distracted, allured and entangled, and the way to you is cut off like a drawbridge pulled up.

Let my signs be prayers.

---

*This is a reference to the famous line near the beginning of St. Augustine's *Confessions*: "Thou madest us for Thyself, and our hearts are restless, until they repose in Thee."

How long will you wait, Lord? When will you come to help me? Please come help me. Without you I cannot enjoy a single day or even an hour. You are my joy; apart from you I sit at an empty table. I am wretched, like a prisoner in chains. Let the sun shine on me again. Give me freedom and liberty. Smile at me, Lord.

Others can chase after what they will, but I want only you. I will pray, and keep on praying, until your kind favor returns and I hear you speaking to me inwardly once again.

I am here, my friend. You have called, and I have come. Your tears and the longing of your soul, your humility and repentance, have brought me to you.

Lord, I have called you and desired you. I am willing to make any sacrifice for you. It was you who gave me this thirst for you, you who stirred the ashes and fanned the flame of my desire for you.

What more can I say to you now? I bow in humility, confess my sin, and praise your greatness.

The Distribution of God's Favors

You are the giver of all we have and are, O God.

If one has received more, and another less, both are yours, and without you there is no blessing at all.

The one who has received the most cannot say that he deserved it or think that he is any better than others. The greatest and the best, after all, is the one who thinks the least of himself and is humbly grateful.

If someone has received less, he must not be disturbed about it. And certainly he shouldn't envy anyone else. Instead he should turn to you, Lord, and praise you for your goodness and your gifts.

You know what is suitable for everyone. You have a reason for giving one less and another more. This is not for us to figure out.

Those who have received less can take special comfort because "God chose the foolish things of the world to shame the wise; God chose the weak things of the world to shame the strong. He chose the lowly things of this world and the despised things— and the things that are not—to nullify the things that are" (1 Cor. 1:27-28).

Four Things That Bring Peace

My child, now I will teach you the way of peace and true freedom.
Lord, I am eager to hear.

1. Do what pleases another rather than yourself.
2. Choose to have less rather than more.
3. Seek the lowest place and be the servant of all.
4. Pray that my will may be accomplished in you always.
Do these four things, and you will surely find peace and inward rest.

My Lord, this short lesson is perfect. With a few words you have struck the target with great force. I can repeat the lesson in a moment, but its truth is gigantic.

Now, if I could simply follow it, I would not be troubled so easily. For whenever I am upset and burdened, it is because I have not practiced these simple rules. I cannot attain it on my own, but you can do all things. Help me.

A Prayer against Evil Thoughts

"Be not far from me, O God;
come quickly, O my God, to help me" (Ps. 71:12).

I have evil thoughts, and I am afraid. How can I destroy them? How can I survive without being hurt?
This is your answer to me:

"I will go before you
and will level the mountains;
I will break down gates of bronze
and cut through bars of iron.
I will give you the treasures of darkness,
riches stored in secret places,
so that you will know that I am the Lord" (Isa. 45:2-3).

Do as you say, O Lord. Let every evil thought fly away from your holy presence.

A Prayer for the Clearing of My Mind

Clear my thinking, Lord Jesus, with the light you shine within me. Chase all darkness from my mind. Check my wandering thoughts and fight for me. Enter into combat with these ugly beasts (my body's appetites), so there may be "peace within your walls and security within your citadels" (Ps. 122:7).

Command the stormy winds to cease; order the waves to be still. Create a great calm in me.

"Send forth your light and your truth,
let them guide me . . ." (Ps. 43:3).

For I am "formless and empty" (Gen. 1:2) until you enlighten me. Lift up my mind. Make me so much at home with heavenly things that it will annoy me even to think of earthly things.

Staying Out of Others' Business

Child, there are some things not worth thinking about. "What is that to you? You must follow me" (John 21:22).

For what difference does it make to you what someone else becomes, or says, or does? You do not need to answer for others, only for yourself. Why get mixed up in such things? I know everyone and see everything that is done under the sun. I understand the dynamics of every situation, and I know each person's thoughts, attitudes, and intentions. All of this is my business, not yours. Don't worry about it. I am not deceived.

False Peace and True Peace

"Peace to you I leave with you; my peace I give you. I do not give to you as the world gives. Do not let your hearts be troubled and do not be afraid" (John 14:27).

Everyone wants peace, but very few care for the things that produce it. My peace is with the humble and gentle, and especially with the patient. If you will listen to me, and act accordingly, you will enjoy much peace.

What shall I do, Lord?

Pay attention to what you do and say. Care for nothing other than pleasing me. Do not judge others or meddle in things that do not concern you. Following this advice will spare you needless trouble. But remember that it is impossible to be entirely free of trouble and fatigue in this life.

Don't think that you have found true peace just because you feel no pain or have no enemies. Never think that life is perfect when you receive everything you want, and never consider yourself my favorite child because you enjoy a great devotional life. That is not the way to true peace and spiritual growth.

What is the way, Lord?

It is in offering your whole heart to me, forgetting your own will in great things and small things, thanking me equally for the pleasant and the unpleasant, weighing all these things in the same balance.

And if you are strong enough to suffer willingly more and more without praising yourself but always praising my name, then you will have the hope of seeing me in the everlasting joy of heaven.

Take Necessities in Moderation

Food, drink, clothing, and all things necessary for staying alive are a burden to a fervent spirit. Let me use such things in moderation, and never prize them too much. I must not renounce them entirely, because you want us to support nature. But to ask for more than enough, and for great pleasures, would be wrong. Guide me and teach me so that I will know when I have had enough.

The Greatest Barrier: Self-love

Give everything to everyone; withhold none of your love. Nothing injures you more than self-love.

Desire nothing illegal.

Own nothing that will enslave you.

Why weary yourself with extra cares? Accept my will and you will lose nothing.

If you constantly search for the perfect experience or the perfect location to improve your life, you will never be satisfied or free from anxiety. In every situation something will be missing, and in every place someone will cross you.

Happiness, then, is not found by increasing your possessions, but by despising them. Renounce your craving not only for wealth, but also for prestige and fame. All of these will pass away with this world.

Your place doesn't matter; your spirit does. You can change jobs and locations without changing yourself for the better, if your heart has no foundation in me. For you will always find again, in the new place, the very thing you were running away from—sometimes more of it!

Accepting Slander

Child, do not be destroyed if some people don't like you and say unfair things about you. If your soul is well-ordered, you won't pay much attention to flying words.

It is great wisdom to keep silent when damaging words are spoken to you. Turn your attention to me and don't worry about rumor and slander.

Don't look for support from the mouths of others. You are who you are regardless of what they say. And you shall know much peace if you neither try to please them, nor care if you displease them.

Call on God When You Need Him

I am in an inescapable difficulty, Lord, and I turn to you for help. Use this bad moment for some good purpose.

"Now my heart is troubled, and what shall I say? 'Father, save me from this hour?' No, it was for this very reason I came to this hour. Father, glorify your name!" (John 12:27-28). "Be pleased, O LORD, to save me; O LORD, come quickly to help me" (Ps. 40:13). For what can I do to help myself? Where can I go without you? Give me patience in this emergency. Help me, my God, and I will not be afraid.

In the middle of this adversity, what shall I say? "Your will be done" (Matt. 6:10). It is not surprising that I suffer, and I ought to bear it. Yes, I want to bear it patiently, until the storm is over and a better time comes. You are able to take even this trouble away from me. You can soften its impact, as you have before, so I will not collapse under it. The more difficult the problem is for me, the easier it is for you to solve.

Recovery

My child, I am the Lord, "a refuge in times of trouble" (Nah. 1:7). Come to me whenever you have a problem. I could help you much faster if you were not so slow in turning to prayer, but you try everything else first. Remember that I am the one who rescues those who trust in me. You will find no lasting help in any other source.

Now that you have caught your breath and your trouble has passed, recuperate in my mercies. I stand near you to repair all damage and to make things better than before. Is anything too hard for me? Where is your faith? Stand strong in me. Have patience and courage; comfort will come in time. Wait. I will come to you with healing.

Are you anxious about the future? What will that gain you but sorrow? "Therefore do not worry about tomorrow; for tomorrow will worry about itself. Each day has enough trouble of its own" (Matt 6:34).

What a waste to be disturbed or joyful about future events that may never materialize! The Enemy will prey on your natural inclination to such anxieties. He doesn't care whether he deludes you to love the present or to fear the future.

"Do not let your hearts be troubled and do not be afraid" (John 14:27). When you think you are far from me, I am frequently quite near. When you feel that all is lost, sometimes the greatest gain is ready to be yours. Don't judge everything by the way you feel right now. If, for a while, you feel no comfort from me, I have not rejected you. In fact, I have set you on the road to the kingdom of heaven.

It is better for you to experience a little adversity than to have everything exactly as you choose. Otherwise, you may become mistakenly self-satisfied. What I have given, I can take away, and I can return it again when I please. When I give something to you, it is on loan; when I take it back, I am not asking for anything that is yours. "Every good and perfect gift is from above, coming down from the Father of the heavenly lights . . ." (James 1:17).

"As the Father has loved me, so have I loved you. Now remain in my love" (John 15:9). That is what I said to my beloved disciples, and you will notice that I sent them out into the world

not to enjoy earthly pleasures, but to do battle;

not to receive honor, but to receive contempt;

not to be idle, but to work;

not to rest, but to reap a harvest patiently.

Remember these words, my child.

Forget Created Things and Find the Creator

Lord, I lack the spiritual maturity to live so that nothing in creation, none of life's pleasures or irritations, can hinder my devotion to you. I know how the psalmist felt when he sang,

"Oh, that I had the wings of a dove!
I would fly away and be at rest" (Ps. 55:6).

Who is more at rest than the one who cares for no earthly thing? For you, the Creator of all things, have made no creature that compares with you. And, unless I can be liberated from a love of created things, my mind will not be free to concentrate on you alone.

This explains why so few of us are contemplative people. Most of us find the requirements too great. We need your grace.

What is not God is nothing. And that is the label we ought to put on it: "Nothing!"

Self-denial

My child, the only way to possess absolute freedom is to renounce yourself. Those who seek their own interests are trapped. They love themselves. They wander around in circles greedily searching for soft and delicate things instead of the things of Christ. They make plans that are doomed to fail because they are not in harmony with me.

Here is my teaching again in a capsule: Let everything go, and you will find everything; stop wanting so much, and you will find rest.

Lord, this is not going to be easy. You're asking for perfection!

Don't be frightened off, my child. Gain an appetite for higher things. I have no greater wish for you than this: that you lose all your selfishness and serve only me. Yes, you have a long way to go. But unless you start the journey, you will never reach the end.

"I counsel you to buy from me gold refined in the fire, so you can become rich" (Rev. 3:18). That gold is heavenly wisdom that sees every worldly thing as contemptible garbage. This treasure remains hidden from many.

Swinging Moods

So you feel one way today! You will feel another way tomorrow. Like it or not, you will be somewhat manic-depressive as long as you live.

Some days you'll be happy and other days you'll be sad,
some days calm and other days troubled,
some days faithful and other days faithless,
some days vigorous and other days sluggish,
some days solemn and other days lighthearted.

But if you are well-taught by the Spirit, you will live above such changes. You will pass through your various moods unshaken and push on toward your goal of seeking me only.

The clearer your target, the better you will weather emotional storms.

Delight in God

I love you, my God. You are all I could ask for. What more can I desire? When you are present, I live in delight. You give me a calm heart, a tranquil mind, and a festive spirit. With your help I can rejoice in all circumstances and praise you at all times.

Nothing is tasteless to those who hunger for you. But nothing can satisfy those who refuse to taste you.

You are the everlasting Light, outshining all created lights. Send your bright beams to penetrate me. Purify and illuminate me with their great power. Give me new life.

Everyone Is Tempted

My child, you will never be free from temptation in your life. You will always need spiritual armor, for you live among enemies who attack at every opportunity. If you don't shield yourself, you will not escape without injury. And if you fail to abandon everything else for me, you will not be equal to the task. Be brave! Winning will be worth the fight, but losing will bring misery and pain.

If you look for rest now, how will you attain heavenly rest? Don't ask for rest; ask for patience.

Be glad to endure everything because of your love for me:
labor,
pain,
temptation,
nuisance,
anxiety,
compulsion,
sickness,
injury,
slander,
reprimand,
humiliation,
confusion,
correction,
and contempt.

These are distressing trials for a new Christian, but they will make you a better person and prepare you for something magnificent. For a brief effort, you will receive an everlasting reward, and for a passing difficulty, infinite glory.

Will you always enjoy spiritual comfort? No, even my most devoted saints had problems, temptations, and feelings of desolation. But they endured it all patiently, trusting me rather than themselves, knowing that "our present sufferings are not worth comparing with the glory that will be revealed in us" (Rom. 8:18). It is ridiculous for you to expect to receive instantly what others have barely obtained after many tears and great spiritual fatigue.

Wait patiently for me. Control your behavior. Take courage and never stop serving me because of suffering or fear. Offer your very life for my glory. I will reward you for it, and I will not desert you when you are in trouble.

God and Your Business

Give *your business to me, my child, and I will make it prosper as I see fit. Wait for me to take care of it and you will be glad.*

O Lord, I gladly give it all to you because my efforts accomplish so little. I wish I did not care so much about success.

My child, sometimes a person grasps and claws for something, but when he obtains it, he finds that some other goal is more desirable. A person's interests often change. True and lasting profit comes only from self-denial, for the one who denies himself lives in freedom and security.

Pride Cannot Be Justified

"When I consider your heavens,
the work of your fingers,
the moon and the stars,
which you have set in place,
what is man that you are mindful of him,
the son of man that you care for him?" (Ps. 8:3-4).

Have we deserved any favors, Lord? What right do I have to complain if you neglect me completely? If you don't give me what I want, what just reason do I have to grumble?

Lord, I am nothing,
I can do nothing,
I possess nothing in myself that is worthwhile,

I am distressingly insufficient,
and give all my attention to trivia.
Unless you help me, there is no hope for me.

Any praise belongs to you, not to me. In you I will rejoice, but as for me, "I will not boast about myself, except about my weaknesses" (2 Cor. 12:5).

Being Honored Is Unimportant

M*y child, do not let it bother you if you see others getting recognition and honors while you are overlooked. Turn to me and the neglect of people will not trouble you.*

Lord, we are blind and insanely vain. Unless I am willing to be totally unrecognized, I will never find any peace within me, or become spiritually enlightened, or be at one with you.

God Is the Best Teacher

D*o* not be led astray by the brightest human minds. "For the kingdom of God is not a matter of talk but of power" (1 Cor. 4:20).

Never read anything in order to appear wise. Knowing answers to difficult questions will not help you nearly as much as spiritual disciplines. Even after profound scholarship, you still need to know me, for I am the Beginning of everything, "he who teaches man" (Ps. 94:10). I will give you better insight than any professor could. I teach without audible words, and without argument and debate. I instruct you to despise earthly things and seek the eternal, to run from honors and endure insults, to place all hope in me and to love me above all things.

Books may contain identical letters and use the same method of communication, but they do not instruct everyone in the same way. The reason is that I secretly teach within each person as I see fit.

A Word of Divine Encouragement

My child, do not be worn out by the work you are doing for me. Let no setback discourage you. I will give you strength.

Remember, you will not be working here forever. If you will wait a little while, things will change. Soon enough all labor and trouble will end.

Keep going, then. Work faithfully in my garden, and I will be your wages. Write, read, sing, mourn, be silent, and pray. Take all blows gladly. The kingdom of heaven is worth all this and much more. When you know the joy of that peace, you will no longer ask, "Who will rescue me from this body of death?" (Rom. 7:24), for death will be destroyed and you will remain with me forever.

A Prayer for Troubled Times

Heavenly Father, the time has come for me to be tested. It is proper that I should now suffer something for your sake. Before time began you knew this hour would come. Outwardly, I will be tormented; inwardly, I will be with you. For a little while, I will be a failure and an object of scorn. Go down with me, Father, so I may rise with you in the dawning of a new light.

Such humbling is good for me, Lord. It helps me throw away haughtiness and pride. It is valuable "that I am covered with shame" (Ps. 69:7), because it makes me turn to you for comfort rather than to people. Thank you for this painful challenge. You know how troubled times can scour away the rust of sin. Do with me as you choose.

> O Lord,
> let me know what is worth knowing,
> love what is worth loving,
> praise what pleases you,
> honor what is worthy in your sight,
> and avoid all that is evil.

As humble Saint Francis said, "A man is as much as he is in your sight, and no more."

Enduring the Desert

My child, you cannot always be spiritually high and inflamed with devotion. You are flesh and bones, and naturally inclined to stumble. As long as you live in a mortal body, you will face weariness.

Bear patiently your exile and the dryness of your mind. The time will come when I will make you forget these painful moments and you will enjoy inward quietness. I will open the Bible for you, and you will be thrilled by your new understanding of my truth. Then you will say, "I consider that our present sufferings are not worth comparing with the glory that will be revealed in us" (Rom. 8:18).

A Prayer for Grace

My Lord, give me the grace that you have showed me is so important for my spiritual health. Let me overcome my natural inclinations. I can't resist these passions unless you help me. "I know that nothing good lives in me, that is, in my sinful nature. For I have the desire to do what is good, but I cannot carry it out. For what I do is not the good I want to do; no, the evil I do not want to do—this I keep on doing" (Rom. 7:18-19). So it is that I start many good things, but then drop out before the job is finished.

Therefore, O Lord, let your grace lead me and follow me, through your son, Jesus Christ. Amen.

Following Christ

My child, the more you can withdraw from yourself, the more you can enter into me. I want you to learn how to forget yourself completely and be comfortable in my will. Follow me. "I am the way and the truth and the life" (John 14:6).

Without the Way, you can go nowhere.
Without the Truth, you can know nothing.
Without the Life, you cannot live.
I am the Way you should follow.
I am the Truth you should believe.
I am the Life you can hope for.
I am the Way that is protected.
I am the Truth that is flawless.
I am the Life that has no end.
I am the straightest Way.
I am the perfect Truth.
I am the happiest Life.

"If you hold to my teaching . . . you will know the truth, and the truth will set you free" (John 8:31-32).

"If you want to enter life, obey the commandments" (Matt. 19:17).

If you want to know the truth, believe me.

"If you want to be perfect, go, sell your possessions and give to the poor" (Matt. 19:21).

If you want to be my disciple, deny yourself everything. If you want a happy life, despise this present one.

If you want to be great in heaven, humble yourself in the world.

If you want to reign with me, bear the Cross with me.

Don't Question God's Judgment

My child, it will be better for you if you accept my decisions without complaint. Do not ask me to defend my actions, or to explain why one person is favored and another seems slighted. The answers to these questions go far beyond your comprehension.

When you are tempted to object, say with the psalmist, "Righteous are you, O LORD, and your laws are right" (Ps. 119:137). "The ordinances of the LORD are sure and altogether righteous" (Ps. 19:9). My decisions are to be respected; they are not to be debated.

And don't waste your time trying to determine which of the saints is most saintly, or who shall be the greatest in the kingdom of heaven. This can cause arguments and dissension, and you may even form parties and admiration societies. The saints would be the first to tell you to stop it!

Some people gather around one godly person, and others gather around another. But this is human love, not divine love. I made all the saints. I gave them grace and glory. I chose them; they did not choose me. I attracted them to myself and led them safely through temptations. I gave them strength and patience.

But I do not reserve my favor for these saints; I love everyone. So, if you look down on the least person, you fail to honor the greatest, because I made both of them and all my kingdom are one, bound together in my love.

When the disciples asked who would be the greatest, this was Jesus' answer: "Unless you change and become like little children, you will never enter the kingdom of heaven. Therefore, whoever humbles himself like this child is the greatest in the kingdom of heaven" (Matt. 18:3-4).

The Prayer of One Who Would Follow Christ

I look only to you, merciful Father, for help and comfort. My soul praises you and seeks to become your holy dwelling place. Let nothing in me offend you. Hear the prayer of your weakest servant who is wandering in a distant place. Protect me from the dangers of this corruptible world. Guide me along the way of peace to my home of eternal brightness. Amen.

PART IV

Preparation for the Lord's Supper

Christ Invites Us to His Table

Christ, the Beloved, Speaks:
"Come to me, all you who are weary and burdened, and I will give you rest" (Matt. 11:28). "I am the living bread that came down from heaven. If anyone eats of this bread, he will live forever. This bread is my flesh, which I will give for the life of the world" (John 6:51). "Take and eat; this is my body" (Matt. 26:26). "Do this in remembrance of me" (1 Cor. 11:24). "Whoever eats my flesh and drinks my blood remains in me, and I in him. The Spirit gives life; the flesh counts for nothing. The words I have spoken to you are spirit and they are life" (John 6:56, 63).

The Follower Speaks:
These are your words, Lord Jesus. You did not say them all at one time, and they are not written in one place, but they are your

eternal Truth and I gratefully receive them in faith. They are your words; I claim them for myself. From your mouth they travel to my heart. They arouse me, for they are tender words of love.

But I am afraid. My conscience hurts me, and I squirm under the guilt of my sin.

Your words invite me to come confidently, but who am I, Lord, that I should dare approach you? How shall I even consider it when I know how unworthy I am? Angels and archangels bow in awe before you; holy and righteous people tremble before you, and yet I hear you say to me, "Come." Only because it is *your* command, can I believe it.

I am stunned. I am about to be the guest not of an angel, but of the Lord of angels! And in your presence I must have nothing in my heart and mind but you.

Then why don't I prepare myself more diligently to receive your sacred gifts? Why am I less eager than the patriarchs and prophets to enter your presence?

If the Lord's Supper were served in only one place, by only one ordained person in the world, many would make a sacred pilgrimage to experience it. But Communion celebrations are offered everywhere.

You come to me, Lord! You desire to be with me! Open my eyes that I might comprehend this mystery. Strengthen me with undoubting faith.

This Communion is health to my soul and body. It cures my vices, subdues my passions, lessens and defeats my temptations. It increases my virtues, confirms my faith, strengthens my hope, and ignites my love. And while I cannot yet be perfect, or as glowing as the cherubim and seraphim, I will prepare my heart to obtain some small flame of divine fire through this living sacrament.

The Beloved Speaks:
If you were as pure as an angel and as holy as John the Baptist, you still would not be worthy to touch this bread and wine. It is not because you deserve it that you should take Communion. Therefore, approach it with respect and reverence.

The Follower Speaks:
When I weigh your goodness on one side of a balance and my sinfulness on the other, I am shaken by what I see about myself. What shall I do, my God?

Teach me the right way. Show me some devotional exercise that will prepare me for the Holy Table. I want to prepare my heart.

The Beloved Speaks:
Examine your conscience. In humble confession and contrition it will be purified and cleared. You must bring no burden that will make you remorseful.

When you have done all you can with such a review, and when you sincerely regret your failures, and turn to me for forgiveness, you shall receive it. "'If an evil man stops sinning and keeps my laws, if he does what is right and good, he will not die; he will certainly live. All his sins will be forgiven, and he will live, because he did what is right. Do you think I enjoy seeing an evil man die?' asks the sovereign Lord. 'No, I would rather see him repent and live'" (Ezek. 18:21-23, Good News Bible).

The Follower Speaks:
O Lord, I simply offer myself to you today as you have commanded. I will serve you forever in humility. Receive me now.

Take, first of all, my sins and consume them with the fire of your love.

And then I turn over to you all that is good in me (though it be insignificant and flawed) that you may add to it and make it acceptable.

I also offer my parents, friends, brothers, sisters—all who are dear to me—and those who have been good to me and to those I love. I bring also those who have asked me to pray for them and for all they love. Protect them from danger; ease their pain; rescue them from evil so they may joyfully thank you.

And I offer prayer especially for those who have hurt me in any way and those I have grieved, innocently or intentionally. Forgive us all equally for our sins and for our offenses against each other.

Take away, O Lord, all suspicion, indignation, anger, and contention and anything else that might hinder the love we need for each other.

Have mercy on those who seek your mercy; give grace to those who need it; and make us worthy to come at last to eternal life. Amen.

The Beloved Speaks:
Clearly understand that nothing you can do will make you thoroughly prepared for Communion with me—not even if you should spend an entire year getting ready, and think of nothing else.

It is because of my good generosity that you are invited to come to my table. It is as though a beggar were asked to join a rich man's banquet and all he could offer in return were humble thanks.

Do what you must, and do it well, not out of duty or habit, but with respect, reverence, and affection. I have called you. I have commanded that this be done. I will give you whatever you lack. Come, receive me.

When I make you glow with devotion, thank me. You are not entitled to it, but I have mercy on you.

And if taking this sacrament bores you, keep praying. Sigh and cry for mercy, and keep on doing so until you have at least received some crumb from my table, some drop from my chalice. You need me in a different way than I need you. You do not come to make me holier, but I come to make you better than you were before.

And it is not enough just to prepare for Communion; let the blessing continue when you have left the table. Guard yourself. Let the small talk go. Find some secret place and enjoy me. All the world cannot take me away from you now. I am the one to whom you must give your whole self. From now on, you must live not for yourself, but only for me.

The Follower Speaks:
Lord God, when shall I be united completely with you, and become lost in you, and forget myself absolutely? I want this devotion more than anything else. I am praying and longing to be numbered with the truly devout.

The Beloved Speaks:
When you feel only a little inner devotion, do not fret. Often, only a small thing stands in the way—if you can call anything "small" that interferes with such tremendous good. If you can just remove whatever it is, and overcome it, you will have your desire fulfilled. I place my blessing where I find the container empty.

The Follower Speaks:
Loving Lord, with all devotion I desire you now. You are fully aware of my weakness, my troubled life, my depression. I come to you for healing, tranquility, and confidence. You know all there is to know about me, even my secret thoughts, and you alone can help me. You know what I need and how great is my emptiness. I stand naked before you.

Refresh your begging servant with spiritual food. Be present with me, illuminating my dark soul. Cut me loose from earthly things and lift up my heart to heavenly things. Don't send me out to wander on my own. You alone are my food and drink, my love and my joy.

With profound devotion and burning love I want to become one with you, O Lord. I hold nothing in reserve, but freely and cheerfully sacrifice myself and everything that is mine to you.

O Lord, my God, you created me and saved me. I desire now with affection, reverence, and gratitude to answer as humbly and devoutly as Mary, the mother of Jesus, "I am the Lord's servant; may it be to me as you have said" (Luke 1:38).

The Beloved Speaks:
Beware of digging too deeply into the mystery of the sacrament and all matters that are beyond your reach. This has caused many to lose their devotion. You need faith and sincerity, not deep understanding of my great mysteries. If you can't comprehend what is within you, how will you grasp what is beyond you? Submit yourself to me and insights will be added to you in whatever measure you require.

Some have difficulty with the Lord's Supper. This is an indication that the Enemy is at work. Do not trouble yourself too much about it. And do not even try to answer Satan's subtle questions. Trust my Word, and take comfort that unbelievers are not tempted the way the faithful and devout are tempted.

I do not deceive you. I walk with the simple, reveal myself to the humble, give understanding to the poor in spirit, and pour wisdom into pure minds, but I hide from the proudly inquisitive. Human reason is weak and easily led astray, but faith cannot be deceived.

For this reason all scholarship should follow faith, not guide it or intrude upon it. I am, after all, beyond human comprehension and I do things you cannot understand.

Afterword

While this reinterpretation has resulted in a considerably shortened version of *The Imitation of Christ*, no essential idea has been omitted from the text. What is missing is the grand style of the original, with the cumulative impact of layer upon layer of repetitive statements relentlessly driving home its central theme of humility. But the gains of this new approach seem to me to offset the losses.

You might want to read one of the complete English versions of this famous book. John Wesley, who produced an abridged version for English Protestants in the eighteenth century, said, "A person will never be satisfied with *The Imitation*, though it were read a thousand times over; for those general principles are the seeds of meditation, and the stores they contain are never exhausted."

Much mystery shrouds the origin of this masterpiece. The earliest extant manuscripts carry no author's name at all. Now that you have read it, you will agree that such an omission is perfectly fitting. The last thing on earth the original author cared about was seeing his name on a title page. However, a manuscript copy dated 1447, about twenty years after the original was completed, does bear the name of Thomas à Kempis, and most copies from then on repeat the claim.

Still, more than two dozen others have been suggested as the actual author, with Thomas à Kempis being reduced to editor. Of the arguments put forward, only two candidates seem worthy of consideration: Jean de Gerson, Chancellor of the University of Paris, and Gerhard Groote, founder of the religious community Thomas à Kempis joined.

Jean de Gerson, who died in 1429, is listed as author on some very early editions of *The Imitation*. A manuscript dated 1460 makes such a claim, and a few printed copies from later years also attribute the work to him. The reasons for rejecting Gerson as the actual author are quite convincing. He was a priest, not a monk. The style, quotations, and themes in this little book are less likely those of a University Chancellor, and more likely those of a member of the Brotherhood of the Common Life, about which more will be said below.

Gerhard Groote, on the other hand, is a serious competitor who is widely accepted as author because of scholarly research in our own time. James von Ginnekin and Joseph Malaise have shown interesting parallels between *The Imitation of Christ* and the *Spiritual Diary of Gerhard Groote*. Groote's troubled life could well have been the source of many hard lessons taught with such conviction. A successful canon lawyer in Deventer, Holland, he suffered a serious illness that helped him recognize the emptiness of his prosperous life. In 1374 Groote gave up most of his fortune, surrendered his lucrative positions, and dedicated his life to spiritual discipline. For three years he lived according to the strict asceticism of the Carthusian monastery. After this time of training and testing, he returned to the outside, preaching to people of their need for deeper devotion to God. From 1379 to 1383 the Netherlands responded favorably to his call to discipleship. But Groote criticized the leadership of the church in the process, and ecclesiastical machinery turned against him. The bishop took away his license and ordered him to stop preaching. Crushed, Groote returned home and lived in obscurity. Others who had responded to his message joined him there and began organizing The Brotherhood of the Common Life, whose members followed a way of life they called *Devotio Moderna*. The Brotherhood grew to become the leading educator of Northern Europe's children just prior to the Renaissance.

Arguing against Groote's authorship is the fact that not one of the seven hundred surviving early manuscripts bears his name. Moreover, none of the Brotherhood's members ever claimed that *The Imitation of Christ* was written by their founder.

After examining the arguments for and against these and many other possible authors, we come once again to Thomas Haemerken (variously spelled Hamerken, Haemerlein) of Kempen, Germany. It is Thomas whose name actually appears on so many early manuscripts. Two typical inscriptions read: "This book was made by Thomas à Kempis, regular at Mount St. Agnes near Zwolle," and "Finished and completed in the year of our Lord 1441 by the hand of brother Thomas von Kempen at Mount St. Agnes near Zwolle." Whether his name was put there as author, editor, or copyist is an issue that will be debated forever.

Thomas of Kempen was sent as a child to Deventer to live and study with the Brothers of the Common Life. He was later ordained a priest in the Roman Catholic church in 1413 and entered a monastery begun by the Brothers at Zwolle. Those were the uncertain days before the Protestant Reformation, and the politics of church and state pressed heavily upon Thomas and his contemporaries. The death of his older brother, of whom he was exceptionally fond, was indirectly caused by the upheaval of the times. If the content of *The Imitation of Christ* requires an author of great sensitivity who had been rocked by overwhelming circumstances, but found peace through God's "inner consolation," Thomas certainly qualifies.

The work is most often published under his name because he qualifies on nearly every point. The discovery of provocative similarities in the writings of others justifies responsible caution in naming Thomas à Kempis as the sole author, but there can be little doubt that he had a major, probably the primary, role in its production.

Thomas à Kempis died in 1471 at age 92, thirty years after finishing the work. He finally found the resting place of perfect devotion that was his life's goal. Marking his grave in Zwolle, Holland, are these words:

"Honori, non memoriae,
THOMAE KEMPENSIS,
cujus nomen perennius
quam monumentum"

"To the honor, not the memory,
OF THOMAS À KEMPIS,
whose name will endure longer
than a monument."

The Confessions
of St. Augustine

St. Augustine

retold by David Winter

Introduction

In the year of our Lord 354, at a town then called Tagaste (now Souk-Ahras) in the Roman province of Numidia (now Algeria), one of the outstanding figures in the history of the Christian church was born. That was Augustine of Hippo. Although not converted and baptized until he was over thirty years old, he became a priest, bishop, theologian of enormous influence, and founder of the Augustinian order.

The Roman Catholic church has always recognized Augustine's importance, but many of the great Protestant reformers, especially Luther, also admit their debt to him as a biblical scholar and theologian. Augustine died at Hippo, where he was bishop, during the siege by the Vandals in A.D. 430.

Even given Augustine's stature as a Christian thinker, it might seem that the life and circumstances of a Latin-speaking intellectual of the fourth century have little in common with English-speaking people in our scientific and technological age. In fact, however, the points of contact are endless. Human beings in every age and culture have asked similar questions, worried about similar problems, and struggled against similar adversaries (most of them rooted in their own nature). Augustine's life story, told with remarkable frankness in his autobiographical "confessions," introduces us to a person much like ourselves.

It is true that the theological questions facing Augustine don't worry many of us today. In early manhood he became a disciple of Mani—a *Manichee*, as they were known. So for many years Augustine espoused strange beliefs about a world of primal forces of light and darkness struggling for mastery. Manichaeism had no room for a personal God and even less for the idea of a God who could take form or substance as the Christians claimed that God had done in Jesus. Augustine was concerned with the relationship between the idea of God and the nature of physical existence—not a common problem today.

Augustine was also concerned with the questions of the origin of evil, which, as he eventually came to see, the Manichees failed to answer adequately. They believed in dualism (that is, that two more or less equal forces of good and evil were competing for control of humanity and the cosmos). Augustine looked into his own heart and echoed the words of Paul, "Who will rescue me from this body of death?" He struggled to contain or overcome temptations, especially sexual ones, but he constantly failed—despising himself, and feeling powerless to do better.

Nonetheless, in Augustine's *Confessions*, we see parallels with modern problems. Augustine lived in a society that worshiped status and success. Often it regarded violence as a source of excitement or entertainment. It gave sports an exaggerated importance and the serious pursuit of spirituality very little importance at all. In Augustine's experience, the group violence of teenagers, self-indulgent sexuality, excessive respect for fashionable opinion, unwillingness to take an unpopular or minority stand on issues of principle, addiction to astrology, and insensitive attitude toward the opposite sex were at different times important influences.

As we read his book, we see the man—and he is a lot like us. Most of the moral problems he faced, we face. Most of the temptations he indulged in, and the issues on which he compromised, are still defeating or compromising us. Where human nature is concerned, there is very little new under the sun.

But most of all, Augustine's spiritual pilgrimage is like ours. He was not prepared to settle for the nominal or minimal Christianity that was widely practiced (then as now). He wanted the best, because he wanted to know God. He would not settle for anything else.

So we follow him along a tortuous and painful path. Slowly all alternatives were closed to him. He was shut in on his search, sensing that Jesus Christ was in some way the clue to it all. Still, for many years he failed to open his mind to the moral and spiritual requirements of the gospel. A brilliant thinker, for long—too long—he thought that the chief barrier to belief was intellectual. Finally, in the climax of the story, a hot afternoon in an Italian garden revealed to him that it was a matter of morality and will. *Faith* is not understanding perfectly, but trusting completely—and being ready to have done with sin.

But that is to preempt a good story. Let me at this point simply fill in enough background to enable ordinary readers to enjoy it.

The church of the fourth century was at a crossroads. After the apostolic period and the terrible persecutions that followed it, Catholic (which is simply to say "orthodox") Christianity had become established virtually across the Roman world. The Cross had had many victories, including the conversion of the Roman emperor Constantine. But those victories carried with them a price. The church, once so distinctive in its message and lifestyle, became part of the status quo.

It still had enemies, and bitter ones, as we shall see. The leading figures in Roman society had reverted to the old pagan religion. Various heresies plagued the church and led the uninstructed astray. For example, the Arians, who denied the physical incarnation of Jesus, and the Manichees are two heretical groups mentioned by Augustine. In many ways it was a costly and painful thing to take one's stand as an uncompromising Christian—as, I suppose, it always has been.

But the church existed, and had power, wealth, and influence. Declining for the most part to take up the Lord's command to evangelize "all the world," it was ripe for the development within its ranks of various superstitions, religious diversions, and philosophical concerns.

In particular, the church of Augustine's day had gotten itself into a strange position over baptism. Most church leaders accepted the idea that sin after baptism was essentially unforgivable (basing the idea on Hebrews 6:4-6). Consequently they preferred to delay baptism as late in life as possible, even up to a person's deathbed, in the hope that he or she would die completely free from post-baptismal sin. Augustine himself never held that view, and later in his life was a leading influence in getting the practice abandoned. He and his illegitimate son were baptized within a year of conversion, although Augustine's father Patricius, a late convert, was baptized on his deathbed.

The church at the time was being pulled two ways: toward the early church, the apostles, and the daring simplicity of their message of repentance, faith, and baptism; and toward a more hierarchical, organized, ritualistic, and legalistic kind of church, in which the primitive message was in danger of being overlaid with new, man-made traditions. Some of those struggles are reflected in the book. Augustine devoted much of his later life to promoting the pure apostolic gospel, untainted with pagan or worldly ideas.

The church of that time was also, however, experiencing spiritual renewal, especially in Egypt, and that movement, as we shall see, touched the life of young Augustine.

But the greatest influence on Augustine, greater even than that of the apostle Paul or the saintly bishop, Ambrose of Milan, whom Augustine admired so much, was the influence of his mother, Monica. If for nothing else, the *Confessions* would stand as an everlasting testimony to the character, courage, and faith of this astonishing woman. In a period of history when women were little regarded except as playthings of young men and possessions of their husbands, Monica never faltered in her belief that her husband and son would eventually share her faith. She prayed and fasted, wept and worried, but most of all she set before them an attractive example of what a Christian could be like. She was quiet, gentle, but single-minded.

Augustine's conversion came in A.D. 386, when he was professor of rhetoric at Milan—1600 years ago. A few of the churches and sanctuaries he knew still survive around the Mediterranean, mainly as ruins. The people who seemed so powerful as enemies of the faith are, for the most part, forgotten, except as names or footnotes in history books. The philosophies that tantalized Augustine, like Neo-Platonism, and the authors he admired, like Cicero, are still available for study, but are hardly regarded as credible bases on which to build an approach to life.

Yet the faith Augustine discovered for himself lives on, in its heart the same today as then: Everything offered to us by God is an unmerited favor—grace—and the means by which we receive it is always complete dependence on God—faith. *Grace through faith* opened Augustine's eyes, as it opened Luther's and Wesley's eyes, and those of many ordinary believers ever since.

Augustine nourished the grace he had received with the same sacrament that feeds us today. He eagerly read the same Bible, especially the Psalms and the letters of Paul, in his early days as a Christian. He was baptized through the same rite. He looked for and experienced the gifts of the same Holy Spirit. He longed for and saw the conversion of his closest friends.

In this paraphrased version of the *Confessions*, much of the original is necessarily omitted. My goal has been to make what in its entirety is a fairly demanding and even obscure book as accessible as possible to ordinary modern Christians. The bulk of the book is Augustine's own story, told in his own words but freely paraphrased into modern English. Nothing is added: what you will read is, as nearly as this writer understands it, what Augustine intended to convey. The later chapters are examples of Augustine's thoughts on various spiritual, ethical, and moral topics.

I hope that this book will be rewarding, interesting, and enlightening. I hope it will be easy to read. What I am absolutely sure of is that its ideals will be anything but easy to put into practice.

PART I

Boyhood

Augustine grew up in a flourishing Roman town in North Africa. His father Patricius was a civil servant, who did not, until his final illness, share his wife Monica's strong and uncompromising Christian faith. Augustine does not seem to have had much respect for his father; most of the mentions of him in the *Confessions* are uncomplimentary. He was, however, grateful for the excellent education his father bought for him at a school at Maduara, twenty miles from his home. That classical education enabled sixteen-year-old Augustine to win a place in Carthage to study rhetoric.

In this section we see young Augustine just before he set out for Carthage. Of course, all the events are viewed from much later in his life. What we have is a middle-aged bishop's account of his experiences as a teenager. That accounts for the sudden little sermons, pointing out the errors and follies of the younger Augustine.

Already one or two traits in his character were emerging. Like many teenagers, Augustine was embarrassed about his awakening sexuality. He did not appreciate his father's jokes about it, and even seemed to think that his mother's attitude was rather lax. Of course, we don't know what he thought about it at the time. But perhaps his persistent anxiety about sex, which caused him agony in later years, began in this adolescent period.

Another distinctive trait is his tender conscience. I don't think that it is simply the perspective of middle age that gives us this picture of a sixteen-year-old who went through agonies of guilt about a few mediocre pears stolen from a neighbor's garden. Probably most of his friends had forgotten about it by the end of the week. But here is Augustine, worrying about it twenty-seven years later.

From that experience, however, he drew some pertinent lessons, even for readers in the twentieth century.

Wrong Priorities and False Ambitions at Sixteen

When I was sixteen, my life came to a turning point. My friends could see I was in danger of falling into immorality, but, far from discouraging me or pointing me toward marriage as an alternative, they seemed to care only that I should develop my skills as an orator and become rich and famous.

My father was neither rich nor famous, but he was very generous with me and paid for me to go away and study in Carthage. I'm not criticizing him and I'm not ungrateful; many parents, much richer than he, did much less for their children. But I have to say that he never seemed to worry about my morals or my lack of Christian faith. Nothing seemed to matter so long as I became "a man of culture." An empty goal.

My father had, of course, noticed that I was no longer a child. All that seemed to mean to him was that I might soon provide him with grandchildren. He was proud of my new virility. In fact, I overheard him laughing about it with my mother—though he wasn't entirely sober at the time, I believe.

To be fair to him, he was only a novice believer, still under instruction as a Christian. But my mother was a mature believer, and she could see the dangers very clearly. She knew I wasn't a true Christian at all and was worried that I would set my life on such a wrong course that I would find it very hard to turn back.

She often warned me, and what she said, I now realize, was the truth from God. Yet even she was not wholehearted in restraining me, partly, I think, because of my father's view, and partly because she also had high hopes of me. Not hopes about my spiritual life, but hopes of fame through learning. So both of them pushed me along the same academic path, my father because he took too little regard of the Lord, my mother because (I honestly believe) she thought my studies might one day bring me to know and receive him. Mixed motives and wrong priorities on their part. Ordinary lust on mine. It was a dangerous mixture, and it did its work.

Why Do We Sin?

When I was about sixteen my friends and I used to round off our evening's horseplay by going to a nearby garden where there was a pear tree loaded down with fruit. We would shake its branches and make off with enormous quantities of pears. Not that we ate them; often we fed them to the pigs. The appeal wasn't that rather indifferent fruit, but the sheer thrill of stealing them. What a picture of human sin.

It's useless denying the sinful component in many everyday things. Gold and silver are attractive to the eye. The touch of human flesh is warm and pleasant. Being praised or exercising power over others can give us a lot of satisfaction. And there is nothing intrinsically wrong with our human capacity for enjoyment.

But we are not entitled to obtain what brings us pleasure by ignoring You, O Lord, or breaking Your laws.

Sin arises when things that are minor good are pursued as though they were the most important goals in life. If money or affection or power are sought in disproportionate, obsessive ways, then sin occurs. And that sin is magnified when, for these lesser goals, we fail to pursue the highest good and the finest goals.

So when we ask ourselves why, in a given situation, we committed a sin, the answer is usually one of two things. Either we wanted to obtain something we didn't have, or we feared losing something we had. Take murder, as an extreme example. A man kills another man. Wouldn't an absolutely typical reason be that he wanted that man's wife, or something else he possessed, and was prepared to kill to get it? Or that he was afraid that the other man was about to deprive him of his wife, or of some valued possession or position?

I suppose one would have to add the motive of revenge, too. But in general we would regard it as incredible that anyone would kill simply for the delight he found in killing. Yet the things we do kill for are hardly ever of the highest order of importance: God's honor, his truth, and his law. Mostly those things are connected with what we might call "creaturely pleasures": the beauty of silver and gold, honor and status in the world's eyes, the pleasure of the touch of flesh, the joy of human friendship and its possessive ties.

Those things do give pleasure, and some of them are good, in a secondary way (and can be fully and completely good, if the obtaining of them is within the Lord's will and according to his laws). But to pursue them for themselves is to commit a kind of spiritual fornication: to seek pleasure selfishly, self-indulgently, and apart from God.

Let's take some examples. Pride struggles to push us to the top of the heap. But the top of the heap is not vacant. God is there, high above all. Ambition drives us to seek power and glory—but the glory and power are Yours, Lord. The promiscuous man or woman is looking desperately for some kind of love in return, but fails to see the love of God, offered freely and without condition.

Some people, on the other hand, seek simplicity and innocence (though sometimes what they are really looking for is ignorance and stupidity). Yet nothing is more *simple*, in the word's real meaning, than the utter consistency of God, nor more *innocent* than the One whose every action is totally opposed to evil. The lazy person is looking for a kind of rest, I suppose, but true rest is found only in God. Others search restlessly for satisfaction in this or that sensual experience, but only "at his right hand" are there "pleasures forevermore." Truly our hearts are restless until they find their rest in You, O Lord. We may confuse being generous with being wasteful, but God, who is infinitely generous, wastes nothing. We long to possess things; God already possesses everything. We grieve because we lose things we have enjoyed. We forget that only in eternity can anything be ours forever.

In other words, sin comes when we take a perfectly natural desire or longing or ambition and try desperately to fulfill it without God. Not only is it sin, it is a perverse distortion of the image of the Creator in us. All these good things, and all our security, are rightly found only and completely in him.

A Double Mercy

How could anyone do what I did: enjoy something wrong simply and solely because it *was* wrong? I stole pears I didn't want, because I enjoyed the act of stealing. Thank You, Lord, for forgiving me all my evil actions.

And I thank You for Your mercy and grace that have kept me from far worse sin, because surely anyone who could sin on so slight a ground—not even wanting the consequences of the sin, but merely the pleasure of committing it—would have been capable of infinitely greater evil than the theft of a few tasteless pears. So I am grateful that You have forgiven me the sins I have actually committed, and also those which I would have committed but, because of Your help, I have not.

How can people have the nerve to claim that it is by their own moral strength that they have remained pure and innocent? Aren't they conscious of their inner weakness, of how frail they are in the face of temptation? In any case, the result of such self-confidence is that they are less grateful to You. They love You less, because they don't appreciate the extent of Your mercy. You do not simply forgive sinners, but deliver them from their sins. Both actions are expressions of Your mercy. It is mercy to the one who does wrong, and also to the one who would have done wrong but for Your grace.

When Company Corrupts

On reflection, I would never have stolen those wretched pears if I had been on my own. It is true I enjoyed the thrill of the theft, but I enjoyed much more the excitement of the gang. I don't believe it would ever have occurred to me to steal the fruit but for the company I was in.

I'm not saying I am incapable of sinning on my own, but in that case there was no personal satisfaction or reward, and consequently no personal motivation. As I have said, I didn't even like the pears.

So what was it about the company that made the action desirable? It wasn't that I was particularly fond of my companions or especially enjoyed their company. But doing it together made it fun. We laughed a lot and imagined what the owner would say when he found out what had happened. We boasted together about the way we'd outwitted him and gotten away with it.

Those things don't happen to us on our own. We don't laugh much on our own, or boast much on our own. But when young men get together, what is at first just a bit of fun easily turns into something cruel, greedy, or vicious. There's no motive or reason for it, often enough, beyond a fear of being different, of standing out, or being thought cowardly. We are ashamed that we aren't shameless.

Again, what a picture of fallen human nature, that friendship and company, which are gifts of God, can be so easily perverted. So friendship itself can seduce us and lead us astray.

But the person who keeps company with You, Lord, finds joy. In Your fellowship there is satisfaction, security, and happiness. Apart from it, as I discovered in those dark and distant days, life is a miserable wasteland.

PART II

Wrestling with Truth

This section covers an important period in Augustine's life, his years as a student in Carthage. There, through the writings of Cicero, he learned that the pursuit of wisdom is more important than prestige or material wealth. That idea never left him, and in fact became the basis of a sincere search for truth that lasted all his life.

But also in Carthage, and when he was only seventeen, Augustine took a lover. A year later, the woman bore him a son, Adeodatus. From that time on—and although at times he despised himself for it—he found it impossible to live without a consort or mistress. He was loyal to his first lover for fifteen years, though later (when he was committed to a wife) he did take another mistress, as we shall see. This "weakness," as he saw it, was a constant burden to him and eventually was the chief barrier to his conversion.

Augustine spent a short time as a teacher in his home town, where the death of a close friend made a deep impression on him. Then, appointed to an excellent post in Rome, he spent several eventful years there with a group of like-minded friends. They all saw themselves as rather intellectual "seekers after the truth," but (as Augustine put it) they "did not see that their intelligence itself was a gift of God."

Manichaeism, which Augustine followed for many years, was a corruption of Christianity that rejected any notion of God being found in material or human form. Consequently, Augustine found the incarnation, with its picture of God taking human form in Jesus, the Word "becoming flesh," totally unacceptable. Manichaeism was only one of a number of heresies that had taken root at that time, and when Monica prayed that Augustine would find his home in the "Catholic" church she meant, of course, the Christian group that had remained faithful to the teaching of the apostles, the orthodox, biblical church that had stood firm against all kinds of strange and transitory ideas.

At the end of this section we see that Augustine took a big step: he turned from Manichaeism. Then in another important new job, in Milan, he came under the influence of Bishop Ambrose and decided to begin a course of instruction in the Christian faith.

The Importance of Truth

When I was studying rhetoric at Carthage I came across a book by the Greek philosopher Cicero. I read it because I'd been told that his language was elegant and his arguments persuasive, and those were skills I desperately wanted to acquire. What I hadn't expected was the effect that Cicero's book would have on me. Without exaggeration I can say that it changed my whole attitude toward life.

The book was called *Hortensius*, and it was really a call to its readers to love wisdom, or what the Greeks called "philosophy." The effect it had on me was dramatic, inciting desires I had never had before. I saw that eloquence—*how* you say something—is much less important than truth—*what* you say. In other words, manner is secondary to matter.

Cicero created in me a great longing to turn from material and worldly things to the pursuit of wisdom. That Greek word *philosophy* speaks of the love of wisdom, and I was stirred up, even inflamed, not toward this or that set of beliefs, but to loving, seeking, finding, and holding onto wisdom itself, whatever wisdom might be.

I was nineteen at the time and was supported financially by my mother, my father having died two years before. She was buying for me the art of eloquence, but Cicero persuaded me that there was something more important than style. At that time I began to rise from the depths into which I had sunk. I didn't know the letters of Paul, or any of the Scriptures, with their warnings against being deceived by false philosophy "according to human traditions," but Cicero warned against those who gloss over immorality with smooth and high-sounding arguments to which they give the name of philosophy.

Only one thing made me cautious about following Cicero's arguments totally: he never mentioned the name of Christ. Although I was not a believer, I had drunk in that name with my mother's milk. So deeply was it implanted in my thinking that I could never be completely satisfied with any argument, no matter how learned or eloquent, that omitted giving Christ a place in its discussion.

So, as a direct result of reading a pagan philosopher, I resolved to turn to the Bible to see what kind of book it was and what it could contribute to my search for wisdom. I came to it at that time, however, with too much pride. The Bible is a book for those who come to it humbly, bowing before its sublime mysteries. I came to it as a critic, and soon concluded that it was not worthy to be compared with Cicero for grandeur of language or ideas.

I did not know then that the Scriptures do not yield their mysteries to proud human eyes. My pride prevented me from humbling myself before them. I did not realize that the Scriptures grow with the spiritual baby inch by inch, and proceed step by step. Simple truths for the simple, profound truths for the mature. I was sure I was mature already, and so I missed the point completely.

A Mother's Dream

When I was a young man, rejecting my mother's faith and disappointing her prayers, the Lord sent her a remarkable vision. It came at a time when she was desperately worried about me; she wept for me more bitterly than a mother who had lost her only son through death. And, in her view, I *was* dead—dead in unbelief, spiritually dead. As a result, she could not bring herself to have me in the house or at the family table. She found my blasphemies and cynicism unbearable.

Then, in a dream, came this vision. She saw herself standing on a wooden rostrum. A young man—an angel, perhaps—approached her. She was overwhelmed with anxiety about me; he looked cheerful and positive. He asked her what was wrong, and she explained that she was worried about the way I was destroying my life by rejecting God.

The young man's reply surprised her. He suggested, as an antidote to her anxiety, that she should turn round and observe where her son was standing. She did, and was astonished to discover that I was beside her on the rostrum. The "angel" pointed out that where she was, I was too. She took his words as tremendous reassurance, direct from God, that he had heard her prayers for me, and all would eventually be well.

I believe it was also from God that she was given an answer to my own rather cynical interpretation of her dream. I suggested that what it meant was that one day she would have the same religion as I (whatever that might be). "No," she immediately countered, "I wasn't told 'where he is, you will be,' but 'where you are, he will be.' "

That answer impressed me deeply at the time, and I often recalled it during the following nine years when I continued to grope my way through the darkness of error and unbelief. All that while, this devout and faithful woman continued to pray for me, more optimistically, but still with a great deal of grief and tears for the life I continued to lead. But her prayers *were* answered, and one day, after nine years of stubborn rebellion, I did indeed stand where she stood.

Breaking the Hold of Astrology

During the time when I was studying rhetoric, I entered a competition for a dramatic poem. Just before the contest I got a message from a medium, asking me what I would pay him if he arranged for me to win. As it happened, I detested the occult and especially the idea of animals being sacrificed in order to procure the favor of the gods.

So I wrote back to him saying that if the prize were made of solid gold, and immortal, I wouldn't agree to a single fly losing its life if that were the price of my victory. I did not take this stand on any Christian ground, of course. Far from it, because in other respects I was as superstitious as the occultists.

That was especially true of my addiction to astrology. I felt that it was somehow better, because it did not involve sacrifices or prayers to the spirits. What I did not see was how astrology also strikes at the roots of human responsibility. It says, in effect, "It wasn't my fault; it was decided by the stars," or "Venus caused it, or Saturn or Mars—not my weakness or sin." It left me, mere flesh and blood and proud corruption, without sin. The Creator of the sky and stars was to be blamed for whatever I did. And who is that Creator but our God, the center and source of justice?

At about that time, however, I met a doctor, Vindicianus, whom I came to admire. He was proconsul at the time, and in the course of his duties he had to award me a prize, which he did by placing a garland on my head. Certainly my head *needed* a doctor's attention, though he did not know it at the time.

Anyway, I was drawn to this elderly man, whom God used to draw me away from self-destruction. He was a marvelous talker. He did not waste words, but had a lively common sense that balanced the serious and lighthearted perfectly.

When he soon discovered my addiction to the stars, his advice was to throw away the birth charts and predictions. After all, he pointed out, I had better things to do with my time than waste it on such frivolity.

He told me about his own experience. As a young man he had intended to make astrology his profession. He had studied Hippocrates, which made the "science" of astrology fairly easy to master. Later, however, he rejected it completely and took up medicine. His reason was simple. He liked to think of himself as an honest man and as such he could not bring himself to make money by deception. And deception was what he had discovered astrology to be. In his words, it was "utterly false."

His advice to me was to abandon it. "After all," he argued, "rhetoric is your profession, and you are well able to make your living at it. You don't have to indulge in this deceitful practice; it's just a hobby to you. So listen to someone who did study it seriously and made his living at it, and gave it up."

I was impressed by his concern, but wanted to know why, if it was such falsehood, it often managed to produce accurate predictions. He suggested that it was pure chance, as irrational as opening a book of poetry and putting your finger on a line at random to find guidance for business or personal affairs. Sometimes, of course, the poetic line seems applicable, simply on the law of averages. But it is demonstrably chance, because the poet had no intention of giving such guidance.

Vindicianus did not convince me at the time. I was more impressed by all the famous and brilliant men who consulted the stars. I found it hard to believe that the whole art was based on chance. But he had sowed the seeds of doubt in my mind.

Some time later I finally became convinced that Vindicianus, and another friend, Nebridius, who were both so skeptical of the validity of astrology, were right. The circumstances in which I came to that conclusion were somewhat strange.

I had a close friend, Firminus, who came to me for help. He was hoping for promotion in his business and wanted to know how I read the stars in this matter. Like me, he was trained in liberal studies and rhetoric, and also like me he was fascinated by astrology but becoming slightly skeptical about it.

I agreed to read the stars for him, but remarked that I was no longer sure that it was a valid thing to do. He then told me about a remarkable incident involving his father.

Many years before, his father and a friend were serious students of astrology. They were so serious, in fact, that they even made a practice of being present at the birth of any creature in their household in order to make a note of the exact time and compare it with the astrological charts.

When Firminus's mother was pregnant, this friend of his father reported that the wife of one of his slaves was also pregnant. They decided to follow these two births with meticulous attention, to compare the two birth charts.

As it happened, the two babies were born at exactly the same time, though in different households, of course. Both were boys, and one of them was named Firminus (who became my friend). But he was aware that miles away in another city was a young slave of exactly the same age, with the same birth chart, who was living a very different life.

That fact bothered Firminus. Why, if they both had the same birth sign and exactly the same astrological chart, should their lives have been so different? He was a wealthy, cultured, successful man of affairs; the other was still a slave, poor, uneducated, and struggling to provide for himself and his family.

But, as I pointed out to him, the situation was more complicated. Here we were, studying the stars to see whether Firminus was destined to achieve the promotion he wanted. But why, if the stars determined that the job should be his, did not exactly the same conjunction determine that the young slave should get it? If there was anything rational about astrology, these two men should have led identical lives, whereas in fact their lives were totally different.

The consequence was obvious. As I tried to read the stars for Firminus, I could either give him a different reading from the slave (bearing in mind his circumstances) or, being true to the art, give both an identical reading, which might prove true for Firminus but could not be true for the slave.

That led me also to think of twins, necessarily born under the same constellation, and especially of Esau and Jacob, in the book of Genesis, who were such different characters and had such different destinies. We concluded that the whole thing was nonsense.

Surely, Lord, the truth is in Your hands alone. No one should say "What will happen?" In Your unfathomable wisdom You determine the outcome of events, the destinies of each individual.

Tears of Bitterness

About the time I began to work as a teacher in my hometown, I gained the closest friend I have ever had. We had known each other since childhood, right through school and university. We studied together and played together, enjoying one another's company and being challenged by the other's ideas and attitudes.

Although my friend had been a Christian from childhood, I set out to divert him from his faith and succeeded, much to my satisfaction. We were, it has to be said, perfectly happy together in our unbelief. However—such are the ways of God—our friendship was suddenly tested. He picked up an infection, and fever spread through his body until he became unconscious. The doctors said he was beyond recovery.

At that point, and without his consent, of course, he was baptized. His relatives presumed that he would have wished to be baptized in the faith of his youth. To me it seemed a meaningless gesture. I had won his mind over to unbelief, so what difference could it make putting water on his body?

Yet, oddly enough, it *did* make a difference. He came out of the coma and seemed to be completely well again, well enough at least for us to discuss what had happened and his feelings about it. As soon as I got the chance to speak to him, I began pouring scorn on this superstitious business of his baptism, assuming he would agree. But much to my surprise he told me to stop talking like that if I wanted to remain his friend. So I stopped, assuming

that when he was fully recovered I would have little trouble per-
suading him what nonsense the whole thing had been.

However, that was not to be. Within a few days the fever returned
more powerfully than ever, and he died.

I was surprised at my reaction. My heart was darkened, and
everything I saw seemed to exhibit the dark face of death. All the
things we had enjoyed together became a kind of torment now that
he was not there to share them. I had no grounds to tell myself to
"hope in God." My only relief was in tears, which came constantly
from the heart of my being. They were tears of bitterness, but they
were also, I suppose, a kind of plea or prayer for help.

Everything reminded me of him: the places we walked in, the
sports arena, concerts, books, meals, even the company of women.
I kept coming back to this desperate sense of loss. I could not escape
from myself, but did the next best thing. I moved from Tagaste to
Carthage. Then, as inevitably happens, time worked its slow but
certain healing, rolling idly around my senses and working subtly
on my thinking.

As my grief passed, I was able to look back to the experience.
Why had it hurt so much? Surely because I had poured my affection
into a bed of sand, loving a person who was going to die someday
as if he had been immortal. What I have learned later, however, is
even more important: The happy man is the one who loves You, O
Lord, You who are immortal and unchangeable, and then loves his
friend only *in* You, and loves his enemy *for* You.

God of Beauty

Whichever way the human heart turns, except toward You, O
Lord, it is wedded to pain. That is true even when it fastens on the
most beautiful things You have made, tree or flower, leaf or bud. All
of those things have both a spring and a fall: a spring, when they
hasten toward perfection, and a fall, when they wither and die. It is
their nature.

What folly, then, to attach our affection to any creature, subject to this law of death. I can praise God for their beauty, but must recognize that they hasten toward oblivion. Indeed, those that more speedily bloom to perfection more speedily cease to be. It is the way of the world, the endless succession of its parts, the one making way for its successor.

"But do I ever depart?" asks the Word of God. The Lord does not abandon what he has made, but is present within it, so that when we find delight in it we are really finding delight in him. On that foundation we can build, loving his creatures, but (best of all) loving him in his creatures.

Indeed, our one true Life, the Son of God, came down to this planet to bear our death, the death of a creature, but through the power of life within him conquered it. He calls us with a voice of thunder to come back to him. And though he has returned to heaven, yet still we can find him within our hearts, present within the life he has made, and giving it new life.

The Eternal Wisdom

When I was just twenty it gave me great satisfaction that I managed to read, and understand, the *Ten Categories* of Aristotle without a teacher. I would mention the book at every opportunity, slipping the title in with a touch almost of awe, smiling to myself when my lecturers would comment how difficult it had been for them to master it.

And much good it did me! Indeed, it was harmful, because it encouraged me to think of You, O Lord, as if You were part of what You had made, instead of being its essence and origin. Sadly, I had my back toward the light and my eyes fixed on the darkness. I could understand without difficulty logic, rhetoric, geometry, music, and arithmetic, but I did not see that my intelligence itself was a gift of God and that all the true things I learned came from him, their source.

What advantage was it to me that I had a nimble wit when all the while I turned from good and clung to evil? Little did I realize then how much better off were all those (as I saw them) "simple" souls who lacked my native intelligence but put their trust in God and sheltered safely within the nest of his church.

A Mother Prays

About that time I was desperately ill, almost, as we say, "at death's door." Had I died, I would surely have gone to hell, my sins unforgiven because unrepented, and unrepented because I could not see how Christ could have borne my sins in his body, since I did not really believe that he *had* a body. I was influenced by the sect of the Manichees, and thought like them of Christ as having a spiritual or angelic kind of body rather than human flesh and blood.

My mother knew nothing of my beliefs, nor for that matter of my illness, but as always she was praying for me in my absence: my absence from home, and my absence from the church to which she was devotedly attached. Looking back, I cannot believe that God could have ignored or rejected her prayers, which were as painful and costly as they struggled from her lips as the childbirth must have been that brought me into the world from her body. How could God have turned a deaf ear to that contrite and humble widow, who was so generous to others, who served the church so modestly, who came every day to the eucharist, and twice every day into the church to pray and to listen to his voice? How could God have closed his eyes to her tears, the tears with which she begged him not for gold or silver, nor for fleeting earthly fame, but simply for her wayward son's salvation?

So in answer to her unspoken prayers, the Lord healed me and raised me up. There in Rome, surrounded by my friends with their strange beliefs, God reached out and touched me. But I was unmoved. My pride was such that I clung to the notion of my own sinlessness. Following the Manichean beliefs, I excused myself of my sins on the grounds that it was not I who sinned, but the principle of evil physically present in me—whereas in truth I am a unity, and it was my own sinful disobedience that created this inner conflict. But at the time, that was something I could not accept. It would have destroyed my self-esteem.

So my recovery from illness did not immediately bring me closer to God. I was, however, taken by the idea, commonly held by intellectuals in Rome, that we should doubt and question everything, because no ultimate truth can ever be comprehended by human beings. At the same time I did not see all the implications of such an outlook. For instance, my landlord was totally devoted to the incredible stories of which the Manichean books were full, but I did not think to warn him to approach them with more skepticism. But I was becoming more skeptical of them myself, or at any rate I did not defend them as ardently as I had formerly.

Sadly, I was completely unwilling to turn to the church for answers, despairing of finding the truth in the Christian faith from which my friends had diverted me, and which taught the doctrine (one I found disgusting) that God himself was Spirit but had taken flesh and blood in his Son. Surely, I felt, that would mean that Jesus, born in the flesh, would also have been defiled by the flesh. The very idea repelled me. But at least I was thinking and questioning. And my mother, God bless her, was praying.

An Important Decision

So I was in a bit of a quandary. I could see, increasingly, that the ideas of the Manichees were weak. They simply had no answer to certain passages of Scripture that Christian friends pointed out to me. They were even reduced to arguing that the New Testament had been falsified by someone (they never said who) who wanted to combine the Jewish law with the gospel. Mind you, they could not produce the original, uncorrupted version.

I still could not accept the idea of a spiritual entity having a physical substance, which meant that I continued to reject the idea of Jesus as both man and God. That kind of conflict went on in my mind all the time that I was teaching rhetoric in Rome.

Eventually I heard of a wonderful post in Milan, one I knew I would enjoy. Evidently the Prefect of the city of Rome was asked to nominate a Master of Rhetoric for Milan, to be paid out of public funds. Some of my Manichean friends were very influential, got me nominated, and paid for me to travel to Milan to take up the post.

As it happened, the job required my working closely with the bishop of Milan, Ambrose, someone I had heard a lot about and respected because of his outstanding ability as an orator. He was courteous and friendly to me, in a fatherly sort of way, and I soon became very attached to him—not, sadly, at that time to his doctrine, which I now know to have been the true teaching of the Bible, but to him as a man and a scholar.

I listened to him preaching with intense pleasure, even though I rejected the heart of his message, which was salvation. "Salvation is far from sinners," of course, and that is what I was then—though, little by little, and largely unaware of it, I did draw closer each day to that salvation of which he preached.

What I began to learn from Ambrose was that the Christian faith could be defended intellectually. It was not, as I had previously thought, intrinsically absurd. I particularly valued the wonderful way in which he explained, one after another, many of the difficult passages in the Old Testament. It was especially impressive to me because I knew the passages well, as far as the actual words went. But because I was spiritually dead I had never been able to understand them. That was a blow to my pride, I suppose, but it was something I had to learn.

So there I was, torn between one set of beliefs, those of the Manichees, which I now profoundly doubted, and another set, those of the Christians, which I had begun to admire but which had for me one impossible difficulty. If I could once conceive of a *spiritual substance*, then the last foothold of the Manichees in my mind would be captured.

I made an important decision. I would leave the sect of the Manichees, because I no longer shared their beliefs. I would become a catechumen, undergoing instruction in the Christian faith, until such time as some certainty of truth came to me. Needless to say, my mother was delighted.

PART III

Marking Time in Milan

At this time, Augustine's mother joined him in Milan. It is impossible to exaggerate the influence this amazing woman had on her brilliant son. Almost equally important was the influence of Ambrose, whose biblical preaching continued to impress Augustine, especially giving him new respect for the Old Testament.

Mental and moral battles continued to rage inside him, however. The intellectuals in Rome had influenced him to be skeptical about the idea of proving, and hence believing, *anything*. Having abandoned the dogmas of the Manichees, he was reluctant simply to pick up another set of propositions, the "Catholic" ones. So he wavered between skepticism and faith, remaining a kind of permanent seeker.

Possibly more important than those intellectual problems, however, was the great moral issue that nagged away at his conscience. He knew that his life did not match his self-image as a seeker after spiritual truth. On the other hand, his pleasure in self-indulgence was gradually slipping away. He found himself neither a confident saint nor a satisfied sinner.

Something would have to change.

Accepting Correction

My mother joined me in Milan, so I was able to tell her that I had rejected false doctrine (which she had for a long while pleaded with me to do) but had not yet turned to the faith she held so devoutly. I know she was pleased, but she was wise enough not to make a big thing of it. It was simply that she had faith that what You, Lord, had promised would come about—not just that I would be freed from falsehood, but that I would be delivered into the hands of truth. All she said to me was that she "surely hoped in Christ that she would see me a faithful Catholic before she passed from this life."

Of course, she said a great deal more to the Lord. I know she prayed even more fervently for my conversion and went eagerly to the church to hear Bishop Ambrose preach. She had come to admire him too, as the "angel of God" whom God had used to bring me to my present open, if wavering, state of mind as a catechumen.

During those days in Milan my mother had an experience that showed me yet again what an amazing woman she was.

In North Africa many of the Christians had a custom, which my mother shared in enthusiastically, of taking cakes, bread, and wine to the shrines of saintly Christians who had died, and there eating and drinking with anyone else who happened to be visiting the tombs. It was seen as a mark of respect and fellowship with those who had died in Christ.

When she came to Milan she decided to honor the shrines of the saints in the same way, and set off with her little basket containing the cakes, bread, and wine. At the gate of the cemetery she was stopped by the doorkeeper, who explained that Bishop Ambrose had forbidden the custom. My mother was surprised, of course, but when she heard the bishop's reasons she quietly accepted his decision. He felt there was a danger of the custom's becoming a disorderly social event, with rather too much drinking. Also, more seriously, the practice had pagan elements in it.

I was impressed by the way my mother was prepared to abandon a custom that had meant so much to her—and abandon it not reluctantly but gladly, once the arguments against it were explained to her. So rather than taking a basket of food to the tombs of the saints she took just her heart, with its holy longings and prayers, and gave the food to the poor instead.

It was an object lesson to me in true humility: the readiness of really mature persons to accept correction, and change not only their mind but their practice. Her response impressed Ambrose too. When we met he broke into praising her, congratulating me on having such a mother. What a pity that *she* had such a son, who could not at that time bring himself to find that way of life and faith that meant so much to her.

My Problems with Proof

I would have loved to discuss all my intellectual and spiritual problems with Bishop Ambrose: he seemed to be the kind of happy man one could talk to. But, regrettably, he was never free. Crowds of people surrounded him all the time, and when he *was* alone he was immersed in study. He never isolated himself, his door was never shut, and there was no secretary to keep people away. But I realized he was entirely occupied with his ministry and with the many people who already depended on him. I longed to ask him what gave him his sense of serenity, how he coped with celibacy (something that was quite inconceivable to me), what his hopes and temptations were, what joy he found in the sacrament, where he found strength to cope with problems, opponents, and disappointments. But I could not, although I spent a lot of time with him. Frankly, the tumult of my mind would have required hours, even days, of his time, and that was not possible.

Still, I heard him preaching every Sunday, and whatever else I made of his words, at least he convinced me of this, that those who scoffed at the Scriptures were totally wrong.

He also helped me by showing that many beliefs held by Christians that I had found incredible or irrational were in fact perversions of true Christian doctrine. One of them, he explained, was an idea held by many of my Christian friends—that, because "God made man in his own image," God also has a bodily form. It was such a relief to find that all the time I had thought I was opposing the true faith I was in fact opposing only a distortion of it.

Mind you, the problem remained. If (as Ambrose said and the Scriptures taught) God is in no way to be thought of as confined to a human body, how could it be that man, who from head to foot is confined to a particular place, is made "in his image"? At the time I could see no answer. But at least I could now appreciate this vision of God, the Creator of all things, filling all things, and not in any way contracted or squeezed into any space or place, or limited in any way by material being. That vision alone moved me to the extent that I began to believe that the truth (could I but find it) lay in the church's teachings.

My trouble was that I could not firmly assent to anything unless I could prove it. I wanted to be certain even of invisible things, as sure of the things of faith as I was that seven and three make ten.

I suppose, having found that the beliefs of the Manichees, to which I had long assented, were false, I was reluctant to be caught again. I was like a person who, having been treated by an incompetent doctor, is reluctant to trust himself even to a good one afterward. I could be healed only by believing. But believing was the one thing I couldn't do.

No Pleasure in Sin

My career was going well, but, in the way things are, that only increased the pressure on me. I wanted honor, wealth, and good sex, but God mocked my ambitions. He made sure that none of those things gave me any pleasure. If he could not (without overriding my free will) prevent my sinning, he could and did prevent my enjoying it.

I was very flattered to be invited to give an oration in praise of the emperor. On the day it was to be given I was inwardly in turmoil, knowing that I was to utter many flattering untruths about him, and be applauded by people who knew that untruths were what they were.

As I walked to the gathering through the streets of Milan, I noticed a poor beggar. He was, I'm pretty sure, half drunk; he was certainly merry. And that was what struck me. I, on my way to this important occasion, was miserable and anxious. He, with nothing to do and no one to impress, was serenely happy.

I commented on this to my companions, pointing out how all our complex ambitions and desires served only to put burdens on us. We strove to be happy, contented, and successful, but we ended up burdened and unhappy. The beggar sought nothing, really, but a few cents' worth of wine, and out of that he contrived a kind of satisfaction.

Well, they pointed out, what he had was not true joy. It was bogus. So was mine, I replied—in fact, more bogus than his. Of course I would rather be in my shoes than his, but even that seemed to me an irrational choice. I was cleverer than he was, true, but he was happier than I was.

Still, my friends said, the important thing is not joy, but the grounds of that joy. The beggar's joy came from alcohol; mine, they claimed, came from a noble desire for glory. But what glory? My inner self protested. Certainly no true and noble glory, nor the glory of God. If the beggar's joy was not true joy, then equally my glory was not true glory. He got his wine by wishing passersby good luck, while I got my "glory" from pride based on flattery. He would sleep off his drunkenness that night. I would carry my guilt to bed with me—yes, and wake up with it, too.

I kept arguing with my friends like that. Of course, they didn't agree, but actually they proved my point by trying to assuage my anxiety with flattery. But it would not be assuaged. My experience at that time, as I resisted God's insistent invitation to me, was the awful realization that I was on a self-destructive course. It made me miserable to admit it. Worse, when for a brief while I found something enjoyable and satisfying, I still could not enjoy it. Every time I stretched out my hand for it, it flew away.

PART IV

Friendship with Alipius

Augustine's closest friend during his twenties was Alipius, a young man who was at first his pupil in Tagaste and Carthage, was subsequently with him in Rome, and then in Milan. He was several years younger than Augustine, but the older man greatly admired his sincerity, judgment, and integrity.

Together they argued out the rights and wrongs of various philosophies of life. With a larger group of about ten friends, they pursued their search for the truth. But it was Alipius who shared some of Augustine's most important experiences, including the occasion of his conversion.

Augustine occasionally speaks of Alipius with hindsight, mentioning how qualities that were latent or emerging in him as a younger man became important in his later life. In fact, the career of Alipius followed Augustine's quite closely. He also was ordained a presbyter, and ended up, appropriately, as bishop of their hometown, Tagaste.

Obsession with Sport

Among the friends I lived with, one of my favorites was a young man called Alipius. He came from the same town, where his parents were leading figures. Because he was younger than I, I several times found myself being his teacher, first in our hometown, and later in Carthage. He openly admired what he saw as my learning and easy disposition; and I admired his promise, both of high moral standards and intelligence.

When he came to Carthage where I was teaching rhetoric, he did not become my pupil at first because of some antagonism between his father and me. What he did become, sadly, was addicted to sport.

The sport in question was the arena, where chariot racing and various kinds of violent hand-to-hand combats drew enormous crowds of screaming spectators. It was thoroughly degrading and brutalizing, but I felt I had no right to intervene where Alipius was concerned. I was not his teacher and did not consider myself then to be his friend, assuming he held the same opinion of me as his father. In fact he did not, but I was not aware of that at the time.

Eventually, however, he began to look in on my lecture and wave a greeting. For my part I was reluctant to say anything about what I saw as his foolish obsession with the games, but in a strange way I was used (by God, I later came to believe) to make him reconsider his addiction.

I was talking about a piece of literature, and an illustration from the arena came into my mind to help explain some point. Without any intention of influencing Alipius, I slipped into a derogatory remark about people who were obsessed with the games. Amazingly, he took this to heart and assumed I had directed it specifically at him. Instead of reacting angrily, as many would have done, he appreciated what he saw as my helpful and friendly warning. As a result, and immediately, he stopped going to the arena and cleared his mind of all the filth associated with those sports.

What was more, with his father's permission, he became my pupil and began to share the devotion I had at that time to the teaching of the Manichees. That continued until he went to Rome—before the time I was there—to study law.

In Rome, regrettably, he had another encounter with the games. The great arenas like the Colosseum drew enormous crowds, people who went there to indulge their lust for blood as the gladiators hacked each other to death. Alipius, in line with his decision at Carthage, kept well away. Then one evening some friends called on him after supper and with mock violence threatened to carry him off by force to the arena with them.

His reaction was typical: He had determined not to go, and his mind was set against it. However, they pleaded and cajoled and half dragged him out of the house, so that in the end he agreed to go, but told them he would sit in the arena with his eyes shut and his mind closed to the obscenities going on below him in the stadium.

"You may think I am physically present with you," he said, "but actually I shall be absent—and that will defeat your plan to get me to that evil event." Those were brave words, but also, as it turned out, overconfident ones.

Alipius and his friends arrived at the ground, where the crowd was already in a great state of excitement, and with difficulty found seats. As he had said he would, Alipius closed his eyes and tried to shut out of his imagination all the noises and excitement around him.

For a while all went well. Then, at the end of a savage fight, a contestant was hacked down with the sword, and the crowd leapt to their feet in a hideous howl of approval. Alipius couldn't resist opening his eyes to see what had happened, "determined to oppose it and despise it," as he claimed afterward. But what he saw affected him spiritually as certainly as it had slain the gladiator.

His mistake, as he realized later, was to have trusted in his own strength to overcome temptation. Now, he could not resist the sight. He was on his feet with the others, baying for blood. He no longer was the decent young man who had high moral beliefs and who despised the decadence and savagery of the arena. Rather, he was a brute, just like the rest, staring and shouting and enjoying the vicious spectacle. What was worse, after that, he went back time and again and persuaded others to go with him.

What he did not know then, of course, was that the Lord would one day call him to the Christian ministry, to preside at the sacrament and care for Christ's flock. Nor did he know that many years later God would draw him away from all these present follies with a strong and merciful hand, teaching him to trust not in himself but in the Lord.

Another Painful Experience

That experience of Alipius in the arena was equaled by another one that happened to him in Carthage, at the time when I was his teacher. Both events, as it happened, were stored away in his memory, and had their value later in life, but right then they were very painful.

One day in Carthage he was strolling through the marketplace at midday, rehearsing aloud something he was trying to learn, and carrying his tablets and stylus. Unknown to him, another young student was also in the marketplace, with less innocent motives. He had brought an axe with him, and by climbing onto the roof of a silversmith's booth intended to hack off some of the lead gratings up there and steal them.

Not surprisingly, the noise of an axe on lead alerted the silversmiths down below, who came outside to see what was going on. The thief realized his danger and scrambled away, leaving his axe on the ground near the booth.

Alipius heard all the commotion and strolled over to see what it was all about. He noticed the thief making off (though he did not know what he had done), and then came across the axe lying on the ground, which he picked up. At that moment the silversmiths showed up and saw Alipius standing there with the incriminating instrument in his hand. Putting two and two together, and despite his protests, they dragged him off to the magistrates, carrying with them the axe as evidence.

His fate would certainly have been a prison sentence, or perhaps a public flogging, had not a certain distinguished architect crossed their path. The silversmiths were pleased to see him, to tell him what had happened, but so was Alipius, who had met him several times in the home of a mutual friend, a senator. The architect took Alipius aside and asked him for his side of the story. Unlike the crowd, he was aware of what had really taken place, and led them, with Alipius, to the house of the prime suspect. At the door of the building was a young slave-boy, too young, the architect guessed, to realize the implication of the question, "Whose axe is this?"

"Ours," said the boy immediately, and that led them to his master, who eventually confessed, much to the relief of Alipius. He went home a wiser young man than he had left it. He had learned, too, something that would stand him in good stead many years later when the Lord called him to be a judge and examiner of many causes in the church. Things are not always what they seem.

The Intellectual Quest

Alipius was one of a small group of friends, about ten in number, who came together in Milan as students of the law. Actually I had met him in Rome, and he had come with me to Milan.

I admired many of his qualities, but perhaps most of all I admired his single-minded honesty. Bribery was rife in the courts there, where he sat as assessor to the magistrates, and the pressure upon him was intense. But he had always despised the giving and receiving of bribes. Indeed, in Rome he had fallen foul of a prominent and powerful senator who offered him a bribe to ease some legal question. When Alipius refused, the man was incensed. He tried threats, but was rebuffed. Then he tried to influence the judge, in whose court Alipius was the assessor. But Alipius threatened to quit the court (and say why) if the judgment went in favor of the senator.

The judge consequently had to rule against him, as the law required, but he laid the blame for the judgment on Alipius, who did not seem at all perturbed at the possible damage to his career.

To set the record straight, however, Alipius might have given way to the temptation to dishonesty over a much more trivial matter. He loved books and study, and once when he was offered the chance to buy pirated copies of some valuable manuscripts at a very good price he was at first inclined to accept. It was a common enough practice.

But he thought it over carefully, as he always did, and decided not to compromise his principles over a thing like that. It was a simple example of the saying of Jesus, "He who is faithful in little is faithful also in much." There is really no such thing as a "little" dishonesty, and Alipius, better than any of us, knew that.

Yet he who was so clear-cut on moral issues hesitated over the biggest question of all. What should be the guiding principle of his life? In that he was in exactly the same situation as I and the other members of our small circle. We claimed we were untiring in our search for truth and wisdom, but we never seemed to find them.

Three of us—the third was Nebridius—made, I have to say, a particularly big show of that search. We did a lot of sighing and heart-searching, constantly asking questions of each other, debating far into the night, waiting at any moment for some blinding flash of light to make it all clear.

Our social life and worldly activities went on, of course. After all, we were men of the world. I had my lover, and they had other pleasures to pursue. *But those things gave no pleasure to any of us.* All we gained from them was bitterness, and all we could see ahead was darkness.

"How long will life go on like this?" we asked each other desperately. Yet it never occurred to us to stop doing the things that contradicted our search for truth—or that a connection might exist between our present life-style and the fact that the truly good life that we said we wanted never actually seemed to arrive.

For myself, I began to despair of ever finding the answer. My search had begun when I was nineteen, and I was now thirty and no nearer the truth, it seemed. Still, I rationalized the situation to myself. "Tomorrow," I would say, "the truth will appear plainly, and

I shall accept it." Or, "Faustus, the great Manichean leader, will soon be in Milan, and he will clear up my difficulties." Or, less hopefully, "Is it perhaps true, as many intellectuals argue, that no certainty is possible in such matters, and the search for it is fruitless? Should I abandon the search?" Or, more hopefully, "I know what I will do. I have already seen that what the Bible teaches is not absurd. I've committed myself to Christian instruction. Surely I should just set my feet back on the path my parents put me on until such time as the truth becomes clear to me."

But even that excellent intention was contradicted by my actions. Like so many people, I enjoyed asking questions and posing as a seeker after truth, but I was pretty reluctant to give that great search the time and effort it really needed. For instance, I had determined to do my academic work in the morning and spend the rest of the day in pursuit of spiritual truth. Fine. But then I began to ask myself, "When shall I have time for my friends?" or "When do I get to prepare my lectures?" or "When do I relax?"

I could see, in my moments of self-awareness, where all this was leading me, but I seemed powerless to change my ways. I knew that the hour of death was uncertain for me, as for everyone, and that to neglect or delay the serious search for truth on such trivial pretexts as parties, leisure, or even preparing lectures was stupid. Logic alone should have told me that the *first* priority was to find God and eternal life, before one became caught up in secondary questions.

But logic didn't. It told me that ambition was honorable. That to become, perhaps, a governor would bring great pleasure and satisfaction. That to be married, preferably to a wealthy wife, would ease at least two problems in life—sex and money. Those, I thought, were the modest limits of my desires. When I had achieved them, I would seriously seek the truth.

While I argued to and fro in that way, with myself and my friends, time continued to slip past. I can see now that although I desperately wanted to be happy and fulfilled, I was afraid to seek the happy life in the one place where it could be found, which in my heart of hearts I knew. So I fled from the truth even while I claimed to be seeking it. I simply did not see that my intellectual problems were really moral problems in disguise.

When the Body Rules the Mind: The Pursuit of Marriage

It was Alipius who raised the greatest objections to the idea of my getting married. I had lived with a woman for several years, and felt it would be more in keeping with my status as a seeker after truth if I moved away from immorality into marriage—not with her, you understand, but with someone more socially suitable. His argument was that he had tried sex in the past and had not found it very rewarding, and that in any case a wife would be a severe hindrance in our search for truth. He lived, it must be said, an extremely chaste life.

However, I argued against this that many of the wisest men were married. It did not seem to hinder them from seeking the truth, or cut them off from God. Not only that, I pointed out, but the real pleasure of sex was not to be experienced in furtive, snatched encounters, such as he had known, but was greatly enhanced when it involved a lasting relationship (such as I had) and would presumably be even more so if given the honorable status of marriage (such as I intended to have). In the face of these arguments, even Alipius began to weaken.

So the business of finding a wife for me began, fully aided and abetted by my mother. She was anxious to draw me away from the life of immorality that she considered I was now in, and she also hoped that when I got married, I might also be baptized.

But one thing was strange about her attitude to the matter. She used to pray to God to confirm to her in a vision his will about this and that (and often she did receive confirmation in one way or another). Yet where my marriage was concerned, although she prayed about it day and night, no such clear vision from the Lord was given her. She managed a few empty and self-induced fantasies concerning my future wife, but she herself knew these were not divine visions.

Still, the matter went forward. A young woman was asked for, and promised. She was suitable in every way, and I liked her well enough, but she was two years short of marriageable age. I had no choice but to wait.

In fact, of course, I did nothing of the kind. My circle of friends had devised an elaborate plan to live together in a kind of community, to further our search for truth together. But the question of wives—some had wives, and I of course intended to be married, broke up the brotherhood, and the scheme collapsed.

While that was happening, I was going through another very painful experience. If I was to marry a respectable young woman I must, of course, be rid of my lover. When I explained this to her, she took it very badly. She could not believe that I, too, was heartbroken to see her go. She felt I had treated her cruelly (as of course I had) and vowed she would have nothing to do with men ever again. She went home to Africa, leaving our son, a young boy, with me in Milan.

I, too, felt I had been hurt deeply, but my reaction was the opposite of hers. Seeing it would be two years before I could be married, and unable to contemplate such a period of abstinence, I found another lover. It was, like all my attempts at that time to find satisfaction apart from God, an unhappy experience. The pain of separation from my former mistress, whom I still loved, grew stronger rather than weaker. It was a dogged, numbing pain within me, completely spoiling all my attempts at replacing it with a new relationship.

The Problem of Evil

At about that time I went through a long period of darkness as I grappled with the problem of the origin of evil. I did not understand that the key to it all was the freedom of the human will. I knew, and clung to the belief, that God was not subject to change or corruption, and that he could not and would not have created anything evil.

So, I wondered, what *was* the origin of evil? If the devil created it, then who but God himself could have created the devil? And if I myself am created by God (who is Goodness itself), how can it be that I so often wish to do evil? Who grafted this evil element into my life? Surely not God. And in any case, could not God, in his omnipotent power, change and convert all the evil in me and everyone else to good? How can evil exist in God's world and against God's will?

Questions like those wracked my brain. I lacked the vital clue that God made us perfect, but gave us freedom of the will; and that we have introduced the principle of evil into our lives by exercising that dangerous gift. Although I could not fully see this, I was more and more convinced of two things: first, that the Manichees were wrong; and second, that when I did find the answer it would lie in the Holy Scriptures and would in some way center on Jesus Christ, God's only Son, and our Lord.

On that basis, it became clear to me that all God has made is good, even corruptible things, like human nature. Because if they were not good to start with, they could not be corrupted: you cannot corrupt something that is already evil. So I could see a distinction. If created beings were the supreme good, like God, they would be incorruptible, as he is. On the other hand, if they were not good at all, there would be nothing in them to be corrupted. They, too, would be incorruptible.

But human beings fall between those two: We are plainly corruptible. So I now saw that as a powerful argument that we were originally made *good*, as the Bible teaches. We are not the supreme good: That is God. But neither are we irreversibly evil: That would put us beyond corruption. But there we are, in the middle, caught in our moral dilemma but unable to save ourselves from it. We are moral beings, made good, in the image of God; but we are corruptible, as we abuse the gift of free will, and are consequently and inevitably corrupted.

More and more, and day by day, I became aware of my nature, because now the Lord was helping me to see it. He began to shine the light of his truth into my life, a light different from anything I had ever known on earth. It was not so much above my understanding intellectually as spiritually.

It was above me because it made me, and I was beneath it because I was made by it. Those who know the truth know that light; and those who know that light know the meaning of eternity. *Love* knows it.

Light Begins to Dawn

I had sought the truth in philosophy and among the intellectuals of the day. I had dabbled with astrology and become a disciple of the Manichees. But at last I began to stop looking at humankind and began to look at God—and I became aware that he was helping me to do it, even though I was not yet fit even to begin to come near him.

It was then that the Lord began to "speak" to me through profound inner convictions.

For instance, on one occasion I became so afraid of the glory and holiness of God that I began to tremble with a mixture of delight and apprehension. It was as though a voice from above said to me, "I am food for the strong. Grow quickly, and you will feed on me. But unlike ordinary food, I shall not become part of you. You will become part of me."

That helped, because I was still bothered by the idea of God being or becoming physical. To me, he was pure Spirit or nothing. So one day I was thinking about this and asking myself, "Is truth actually nonexistent, seeing it is not part either of finite or infinite space?" And again the Lord spoke to me, as though from a vast distance, "Yes, there *is* truth: *I am who I am.*" I heard that, not with my ears, but, as they say, in the heart. It convinced me, so that I could never again doubt it, that truth exists and can be clearly seen and understood through what God has made, including human beings.

That experience led me to reflect on all the created things under God. I saw that none of them had any absolute being (because all were subject to time, decay, death, or destruction), but also that none of them had absolutely no being at all. They existed, but not, as it were, in their own right. All of them depended on God. They exist *only* because he exists. But their existence is not absolute, because they are not what God alone is—eternal. So every creature has a being because he is made by God, but no creature has an absolute being, because he is not what God is.

From such an awareness I drew a clear conclusion. It would be wise for me to hold fast to God, because apart from him I too have no absolute being. But in him I can be what he is, as indeed he had "told" me earlier.

Then came another insight, based on a common experience in daily life, but very revealing to me at that moment. The same bread that is pleasant and refreshing to a healthy man can be nauseating to a man who is sick; the sunlight, which is glorious to the person with sound eyes, is intensely painful to sore or tender eyes. So I realized that God's justice, which is pleasant and refreshing to those who love his ways, may well be offensive and evil to those who reject him. That understanding seemed to shed light on my continuing struggle with the problem of evil. Surely it could have its origin not in any thing or substance, but in a perversion or swerving away from God, a sort of deflection of the will toward lower things, so that the goodness of God finally seems evil, and evil, good.

The trouble was that those thoughts, which I truly believe came from God, drew me toward him, but my body and its desires instantly pulled me away again. I never doubted now that the Lord himself was the one to whom I ought to commit myself, but I simply could not do it. My mind raised endless questions, and those questions God in his mercy patiently answered. But my body raised questions too, and it seemed to me at that time to be stronger than the spirit. After all, it is through the body and its senses that we perceive things at all. The problem for me was that those very senses were distorting my perception of the truth.

So I took another approach. I felt that my reasoning faculties were being corrupted by my bodily senses—for instance, whole processions of sensuous images could march across my mind whenever it tried to raise itself up to spiritual and divine things.

Yet my mind knew, and cried out, that it preferred the unchangeable to the changeable. For a moment on one occasion it raised itself above my habitual sensuality, opening itself to the light. In a blinding flash of insight, at once marvelous and terrifying, my mind saw *"that which is"*: the great inner reality of existence. The "invisible things of God, which are understood by the things that are made." The "substance of things hoped for, the evidence for things not seen."

But I could not hold my eyes on the sight. In a moment or two I was simply looking again at the familiar objects around me. My wonderful experience was only a precious memory, the distant savor of a meal I had seen from afar but had not been able to eat.

Misconceptions about Jesus

My view of Jesus was of a man of perfect wisdom far above all other men, but himself not more than a man. I gave him supreme authority as a master, and was greatly impressed by the idea of his virgin birth, which intrigued me by its example of the priority of spiritual over physical things. But I could not see what naturally follows from this, that "the Word was made flesh."

As I saw it, Jesus' life was one in which the Word of God was perfectly present, his soul and mind working in perfect harmony. All that I read about him in the Scripture—his rejoicing and sadness, his deeds and preaching—led me to acknowledge that Christ was a complete and perfect man. I could not yet conceive that he was the truth of God *in person*, but I did believe that above all others he *conveyed* the truth of God.

My friend Alipius, on the other hand, had the opposite difficulty. He thought that Christians believed that, in the incarnation, God became human in such a way that there was neither the soul nor the mind of man in Jesus. All there was was God . . . and flesh. The difficulty such a belief raised for Alipius is obvious. How could Jesus perform the things we read in the Gospels unless he were a living, thinking human being, a man with soul and mind?

So, because he thought that Christians denied it, Alipius moved more slowly and reluctantly than I did toward the faith. Later, of course, both of us realized how wrongly we had grasped the truth about Christ. Surprisingly, perhaps, Alipius realized the fact before I did. It was a long while before I came to understand what the true Christian teaching was about "the Word made flesh."

My basic trouble was an obsession with being intellectual, or appearing to be so, puffed up with my own cleverness. I expected God to reward my "wisdom." But where was my humility? Where was my love of God, who owed me nothing? I seemed to be two people, one wanting to be right with God, the other just wanting to be right.

It was then that the apostle Paul came to my aid. I had determined to read again all his books, and I found they spoke with amazing relevance to my position. Here, in the letter to the Romans, for instance, Paul faced questions that the Platonists and other philosophers never even asked. But they were questions that tormented me. When I read those verses, they seemed to echo my own despairing cries: "My mind delights in the law of God, but I see another law at work in my body, which rejects it, and leads me captive to the law of sin which resides in my body. Who shall deliver me from this body of death?" And then came the answer. "I thank God, through Christ Jesus our Lord."

The books of the philosophers never speak of such inner conflicts. They do not tell of troubled spirits, of "a broken and contrite heart." No one lifts his voice in their pages to sing out, "Shall not my soul wait on God, for from him comes my salvation . . . He is my God and my Savior, my Protector. I shall never more be moved." In their books you will not hear a voice saying, "Come to me, all you who labor and are weary"—because they despise anyone who is, as Jesus claimed to be, "meek and humble of heart." Why are such things not found in their writings? Because God "has hidden them from the wise and learned, and revealed them to babes."

As I read Paul's words, and the other words of Scripture, I realized in a clearer way my position. It was one thing to sit, as I had done, on some wooded mountaintop and view the land of peace far away, without knowing the way there or being able to overcome the impenetrable barrier raised by error and sin. It was quite another thing, and infinitely better, to leave that apparently secure mountaintop and, trusting God to lead the way, walk securely toward the land of peace. At last, at last, I felt I was on the journey.

PART V

The Moment of Truth

Augustine's conversion occurred when he was thirty-two, so the process that led to it was a long one. His account of the days leading up to it, and the actual event itself, is one of the great spiritual testimonies of Christian history. From his prayer that God would "make him holy ... but not yet," to the moment when some children chanting a playground rhyme drove him to open his copy of the letters of Paul, his story has all the qualities of a devotional classic. Yet all is told with disarming modesty. Augustine makes no attempt to gild the lily.

A number of distinguished names play a role in the story. Ambrose was one of them, the bishop of Milan whose hymns are still sung today. Another was Simplicianus, who prepared Augustine for baptism. He was for many years Ambrose's assistant, and after the great man's death, when Simplicianus himself was an old man, he succeeded Ambrose as bishop of Milan.

But a decisive influence was that of a layman, a new convert. Marius Victorinus was a noted intellectual of the time, a distinguished Neo-Platonist and rhetorician. His conversion to Christianity, and especially his public confession of it, caused a great stir in Milan and evidently contributed to the repentance of the still-wavering Augustine.

The Last Steps:
The Power of Testimony

I had reached the point of no return. The word of the Lord penetrated to the root of my being. I felt that God was boring in on me on every side, giving me no way of escape. I no longer had doubts about the eternal life of God, nor about the relationship of physical substance to spiritual being. In my head I was converted. I could find no argument against the truth. Yet where my earthly life was concerned, everything remained unresolved. My heart was still contaminated with the subtle influences of the world and the flesh. Try as I would, I could not imagine life without sexual gratification. I could find no fault in the One who is the Way, the Savior of the world, but I could not bring myself to follow him through the narrow gate that leads to life.

At that point God directed me toward an old and wise man, Simplicianus, a person who from his youth had led a devout Christian life. It was he who had led Bishop Ambrose to the Lord many years before. Now, in his old age, he seemed to me to have the long experience and spiritual discernment that could guide me through my present confusion.

So I went to him, and explained my dilemma: how I had come through many experiences and setbacks to this situation, that I no longer found any satisfaction or pleasure in worldly success or acclaim, that I was disgusted with my own way of life and especially that my body so often ruled my will, that nothing any longer gave me the joy that the Lord did. But, I added, I was trapped by sexual lust, and, being morally weak, constantly chose the soft and easier option.

In short, I said, I knew now that I had found the "pearl of great price" of which Jesus spoke, but I doubted whether I was prepared to pay the price of acquiring it.

Simplicianus listened and then, instead of answering my questions, picked up a passing reference I had made to the works of a famous master of rhetoric in Rome, Victorinus, whom I believed had died a Christian.

Simplicianus saw at once that my problem was my unwillingness to humble myself, or to believe that the truth is hidden from human wisdom but revealed to babes. For that reason he began to tell me the story of how Victorinus came to Christ.

Victorinus was one of the most outstanding scholars of the time, distinguished in the liberal sciences, a respected student and critic of the great philosophers, a tutor to many of the most noble senators. For all those services in high office he was marked out for an unusual honor: his statue was erected in the Forum in Rome.

All his life he had been a worshiper of idols and a devout follower of pagan religion, as, in fact, were almost all the leading figures in Rome at that time. Indeed, he championed the cause of old religions with thunderous eloquence.

Later, in his old age, Victorinus began to study the Holy Scriptures and to seek out and pore over other Christian writings. He found them enormously attractive and convincing, so much so that he came to Simplicianus privately and said, "I would like you to know that I have become a Christian." Simplicianus, however, was not readily convinced of that.

"I will never believe it, nor accept you as a Christian, until I see you publicly in the church of Christ," he said.

Victorinus laughed. "So it's the walls of the church, then, that makes people into Christians?"

But Simplicianus stood his ground for many weeks, the elderly intellectual claiming that he was indeed a Christian, and the Christian minister saying that he was not a Christian until he was prepared to join the visible body of Christ. Often Victorinus would end the argument with his remark about the church's walls. The truth was, as he well knew, that he was afraid to offend his friends, the followers of the pagan gods, who might turn against him if he renounced their religion and acknowledged Christ publicly.

Eventually Victorinus came across the warning of Christ in the Gospels, that he would not confess before his holy angels those who were afraid to confess him before men. The old man began to fear that he might in the end be denied because of his unwillingness to confess Christ publicly. He also saw that it would be a grievous thing formerly to have joined in the sacrilegious rites of the pagan temple freely and proudly, but now to have refused to receive the sacraments of the church humbly, as bearers of the Word.

So he surprised Simplicianus one day by saying, "Come on, let's go to church. I am resolved to be a Christian." Delighted, Simplicianus went with him to church, where he was enrolled for instruction in the faith. Soon he turned in his name as a candidate for baptism, intending to demonstrate his new birth—both to the amazement of the people of Rome and to the joy of the Christians.

When the day came for his profession of faith in baptism, the priests made an offer to Victorinus of a more private ceremony to spare him too much public attention (a concession that occasionally was offered in suitable circumstances). But he refused, saying he would rather profess his faith in the presence of the whole assembly. After all, he said, what he had taught in the past was public knowledge. Why should this much greater matter of salvation not be confessed publicly?

When he rose up to make his profession (which at Rome was done in a set form of memorized words), the whole congregation recognized him. "It's Victorinus!" they whispered to each other across the church. For a moment they could not contain their surprise and pleasure, but shouted out for joy. But as he began to speak, the congregation hushed, not wanting to miss a single word. He declared his faith before them with great confidence, and instantly the whole congregation took him to their hearts.

A Chain of Iron

The story Simplicianus told me had exactly the effect he had hoped for. I was suddenly burning with desire to follow the example of Victorinus. Later, during the time of the Emperor Julian, Simplicianus told me Victorinus had to choose whether to continue to teach rhetoric or to concentrate on the Scriptures, since an imperial edict now forbade Christians to teach literature or rhetoric. Of course Victorinus chose the way of God's Word. I counted him blessed, rather than resolute, to be able so easily and clearly to settle the issue.

I longed that I might be given a similarly clear choice. I felt myself bound by a chain of iron, a chain forged by the Enemy out of my own unruly will. What happens to us is that impure desires spring from our misdirected affections, and by giving in to them we create a habit, which in turn becomes a kind of necessity. That process bound me like the links of a chain. My newfound will, which longed to serve God, was not yet strong enough to overcome my old corrupted will, hard tempered by long practice. So my two wills struggled—the new against the old, the spiritual against the carnal—and in the process nearly tore my spirit apart.

That was just what the apostle Paul had said. "The flesh lusts against the Spirit, and the Spirit against the flesh." I was experiencing what he and others had experienced before. I was not unique.

The trouble was quite simply a failure of my will. I was like a sleeper who wakes and fully intends to get up and get on with the day's activities, but in fact turns over for another nap. My mind was convinced, but my body would not follow its signals. On every side the Lord showed me what I should do, and all I could say in response was "Yes, yes, I agree. Soon. I shall do it very soon. Have patience with me just a little while longer." But in fact the *soon* grew longer and longer and the *little while* stretched out into a long while.

I found that the law of habit is a vicious one, a kind of "law of sin," which can hold the mind of human beings even against their will. We pay a heavy price for having first slipped into sin so willingly. As my favorite apostle put it, "Wretched man that I am, who shall deliver me from this body of death?" I knew, as he knew, that the only answer was the grace of the Lord Jesus Christ.

Make Me Holy . . . But Not Yet

The story of Victorinus had a great effect on me, but it was reinforced by an experience a few days later. Alipius and I were visited by a friend from Africa, Pontitianus. He had a high position in the emperor's household. I cannot remember what the occasion of his visit was, but I can vividly recall his picking up my book of Paul's epistles, which I had by me on the table. He seemed pleased to see it there and a bit surprised. When I explained I was giving a great deal of time to the reading of Scripture, he took the opportunity to explain that he was a Christian and recently had the opportunity to study the works of an Egyptian monk, Antony. Neither Alipius nor I had ever heard of him nor of the great spiritual revival that had followed his ministry. Thousands of men had entered the monasteries to give their lives to prayer and service, even in the heart of the desert.

More than that, Pontitianus told us, there was a flourishing monastery here in Milan, just outside the city walls, under the pastoral care of Ambrose. We, who lived in Milan, knew nothing of it.

He then went on to tell how he had been on a visit to Treves, with three other agents in public affairs, while the emperor was at the afternoon games in the circus. The four had split into twos and were walking casually near the town when the other two men came upon a poor cottage, where several devout Christians live in complete self-denial. They were "poor in spirit," who shall "inherit the kingdom of heaven."

There they were shown a book of the life of Antony, which one of the companions of Pontitianus began to read. Doing so, he was overcome with determination to lead a similarly dedicated life, not "one day," or "soon," or "in a little while," but there and then. He explained his intention to his friend, saying he had decided to break with his present life and ambitions and join this little community immediately—without even returning to town. His friend, to his surprise, said he would join him.

When Pontitianus and his companion caught up with them, they tried to persuade them to return to the emperor's court. But when they saw how sincerely convinced the two of them were they tearfully congratulated them, promised to support them with their prayers, and rather reluctantly made their way back to the palace.

The first two, filled with a new vision, remained in the poor cottage. Both of them, as it happened, were engaged to be married, but when their fiancees heard what had happened, they also decided to give their lives to God's service and entered a community.

Just hearing that story was a hideous rebuke to me. It forced me to look at myself and to hate what I saw. For so many years, ever since I was nineteen, I had claimed to be searching for the truth. Yet here I was, still delaying, still putting it off, while these men had responded to God's call instantly—not over years or months or even weeks, but within *minutes*. From my teens I had prayed to God for purity, it is true. But I had always added a qualifier. "Lord," I would pray, "make me content, but not yet." I was afraid that God would instantly answer and instantly deliver me. What I really wanted was not that my lust should be quenched so much as glutted.

I had fooled myself that I put off making a decision because I was not sure which was the right way to go. Yet here I was, absolutely sure of the way, convinced of the truth, and yet still prevaricating, still praying, "Lord, make me holy . . . but not yet."

One Day in the Garden

There was a garden to our lodging, which we had free use of since the owner of the house lived elsewhere. One day, during this period of my spiritual turmoil, I made my way into the garden accompanied by Alipius. I felt I had arrived at a crisis. My voice was strained and strange, my face flushed, and tears were beginning to wet my cheeks.

"Look," I said to Alipius, "look at the state we are in. The uneducated and simple are committed Christians, and we, with all our learning, are still trapped by flesh and blood."

We sat as far from the house as possible, I groaning and weeping, he surprised and anxious. I now could see that everything came down to a problem of the will. We can do nothing unless we will it, from raising a hand to setting out on a journey over land and sea. We must have the will to do it, a determined and strong will, not a halfhearted, ambiguous, indecisive one.

Where our bodies are concerned, unless there is some physical weakness or deformity, the will and the power to do something are virtually one and the same. I think of lifting my hand, and I do it.

Why, then, I wondered, was it that the mind itself was so slow to obey the will? Could it be because when we will a simple physical movement we will it *entirely*, the means and the end, whereas when we will a spiritual or moral issue, we may will it only in part, or halfheartedly? Is it then the indecisiveness that thwarts the action? We do not do it because deep down we are not sure we want to do it.

So I sat there in the garden, in a private world of my own. My old nature, the body of death which I had inherited as an heir of Adam and his sin, struggled to retain a hold on me, while the Lord redoubled his inner call to me to have done with this old nature and rise to a new one. I kept saying to myself, "Come on, let it happen now, let it happen *now*," and as I spoke I almost resolved to do it. But I did not. Yet I did not slide back into my old nature either. It was as though I stood outside myself and watched the struggle. I was hanging there suspended between dying to death and living to life. I was surprised how powerful was the restraint of my old evil habits and how subtly they tugged at me, holding me back.

"Just think," they whispered, "if you take this step, you will never again experience the pleasures of sexual indulgence. From that moment, all those things will be forbidden you forever. Can you really live without us?" And although I knew they were merely toys and frivolities, compared to eternal values, their voices were insistent and their appeal held me back.

But it was a dwindling power; nothing like it had been on previous occasions. It was as though I could see in front of me a better vision, a picture of a whole new kind of life, a life of purity and self-discipline. Nor was it a gloomy or negative scene. Far from it. It was actually enticing, but not in a dissolute way. I could see, in the vision, scores of people of all ages, young men and women, elderly widows, older men, but all of them smiling and welcoming, apparently overflowing with inner joy.

A voice said to me, "Can't you do what all of these people have done? And yet, *they* have not done it, certainly not in their own strength. They have come to this joy through a strength given to them by the Lord their God.

"Your trouble is that you are trying to achieve such a state in your own strength, and consequently you are achieving nothing at all. Cast yourself on God alone and trust him. He will not hold back and let you fall. But you have to trust him completely. Then, and only then, will he receive and heal you."

I hesitated, hearing again those malicious whispers in my ear. "Can you really live without us forever?"

But the heavenly voice spoke again. "Close your ears to those murmurs. They come from your fallen, sinful nature. Put it to death. I know they speak to all kinds of sinful delights, but they are contrary to the law of the Lord your God."

That strange debate went on within me, while poor Alipius sat at my side waiting silently for the battle to be resolved.

At that point I needed to be alone, and I said something to that effect (I can't remember the words) and left Alipius, so that there was no human restraint on me at all. I flung myself to the ground under a fig tree and wept bitterly, a "sacrifice acceptable to You, O Lord." I cried out loud, in some such words as these: "How long,

Lord? How long? Will You be angry with me forever? Do not remember my former sins."

It was indeed those former sins and their present power that seemed to be holding me back. So I went on praying. "How long, Lord? Tomorrow and tomorrow? Why not now? Why not at this moment make an end of my uncleanness?"

Then, as I prayed, I heard a voice, like a little boy or girl in a nearby house, repeating some words by heart in a singsong manner: "Take it up and read it. Take it up and read it."

I was arrested by the sound. I had never heard those words used in a children's game. My bitterness and tears stopped. I got up, convinced that the message was from heaven and that it was telling me to read from the first chapter I should find on opening my book of Paul's writings. I remembered how Antony had been told—in a rather similar way, by a passage in the Gospels that was apparently meant for him at one point in his life—"Go, sell all you have, and give to the poor, and you shall have treasure in heaven. And come, and follow me."

So I went back to the table where Alipius was sitting and picked up the book of Paul's writings which I had left there. I took it quickly in my hand, opened it, and read silently from the chapter that my eyes first lighted on. "Not in orgies and drunkenness, not in promiscuity and lust, not in anger or jealousy: but put on the Lord Jesus Christ, and make no provision for the flesh and its desires."

I needed to read no further. Instantly, as I reached the end of the sentence, all the darkness of my former doubts was dispelled, as if a clear and insistent light had flooded my heart. I must turn from the old; I must put on the new; and I must do it now.

I shut the book, though marking the page, and told Alipius in a quiet and calm voice exactly what had happened. In his turn, he told me what had been going on in his own heart, which I knew nothing about. He then asked if he could see the passage I had read—but he read on a little further to some words I had not known were there. "Now him who is weak in the faith take with you." He applied this to himself, he told me, and at once without any hesitation, he joined me in my newfound purpose and commitment.

Immediately we went into the house to find my mother and tell her what had happened. Needless to say, she was overjoyed. As she said, the Lord is "able to do more abundantly than we either ask or think." She said that because she had limited her prayers to my conversion. But so deeply had God worked in me that I had instantly forsaken all human ambitions, even the desire for a wife, and had decided to dedicate myself to that very rule of life which the Lord had shown my mother many years before that I should accept, an acceptance which even she had scarcely the faith to believe would ever actually happen.

PART VI

Believing . . . and Grieving

Augustine's conversion brought him great joy and a sense of relief, but it seems safe to say that it gave equal joy to his mother. His baptism, together with his son Adeodatus, and best friend Alipius, was an occasion for celebration. Sadly for Augustine, that event was quite soon followed by his mother's death, which proved a severe test of his newfound faith.

The *Confessions* end there. The prodigal had come home. The one who had watched over and prayed for him all his life had gone to her rest contented.

Of course there is much more to the life of Augustine. He founded a monastic order, still with us today. He was ordained presbyter in A.D. 391 by Bishop Valerius of Hippo. Then, when the bishop died four years later, Augustine was appointed in his place. He exercised an enormous influence on the church of his day, training clergy (twelve of his men became bishops in Africa) and writing a formidable number of books to refute heresies and argue the case for apostolic Christianity.

The Effect on Our Friends

The first decision I made after my conversion was to forsake as quickly as possible the profession and teaching of rhetoric. I saw now that it was little more than a matter of marketing a lying tongue: using the gift of eloquence not to serve law and peace, but to win legal battles. My conversion happened about three weeks before the end of the school term, and although it was painful to do so, I felt that in fairness to my pupils I ought to complete the term's work.

I say *painful*, and it was that in two senses. Spiritually, because all desire for money-making had gone from me, and that was really the main motive in the whole business. But also physically, because I had some trouble with my lungs, which made breathing almost impossible. That circumstance, however, gave me a completely valid excuse to limit my teaching and other work, and thus made the whole process easier. It also helped me avoid the apparent ostentation of announcing that, having become a Christian, I was abandoning my highly paid and prestigious post.

My mind was set free from the biting cares of ambition and wealth, and also from the temptations of impurity and lust. I simply sat in my room and prattled away to the Lord like a talkative child.

Our two friends and companions, Verecundus and Nebridius, had not, of course, shared our experiences in the garden. Verecundus was the more upset, because he saw that it would end our association. He was drawn toward the faith, but although his wife was a Christian, he saw her as the main stumbling block in the way of his conversion. That was because, as he put it, "I don't want to be less of a Christian than you two, and that I can't be as a married man."

We tried to reassure him, telling him he could be totally faithful to Christ in his present married state. But at that time he could not be persuaded.

He was kind enough to lend us his country house at Cassiciacum, however, and there we were able to live while we worked out the implications of our conversion. Later on, in our absence, he became ill, but in that sickness, which proved fatal, he became a true Christian. We took this in one way as a sign of God's mercy to him and to us. Certainly we should have been distraught, had he, who had been so close to us, died outside the faith.

Nebridius also came to Christ. He had been caught up in that detestable heresy which believed that Jesus did not truly take human flesh, but was only a spiritual being on earth. But at the time of our conversion he was fighting free of that delusion and was genuinely seeking the truth. Soon after, he too was converted and subsequently led all his household in Africa to Christ. But then, like Verecundus, he was taken ill and died, and lives now in paradise.

I remember him with love and delight to think that he is indeed living with the Lord as a true son in the heaven he often used to ask me about—me, who was then as ignorant as he was of spiritual things. Now he has no need to bring his questions to so inept and inexpert a guide, but can drink wisdom to the full from the well-spring of all knowledge. And I dare hope that he also remembers me.

The Joy of the Spirit

When the school term ended, I was able to dedicate myself to filling my heart, too, with spiritual riches. I wrote many letters, some of them to dear Nebridius, trying to explain what God had shown us and bearing testimony to his grace in our lives. And the Lord worked on me, on all my roughness and pride, subduing and humbling me, sometimes with sharp goads, sometimes with blessings that made me rejoice.

I rediscovered the Psalms of David, those wonderful hymns of faith, whose words rebuke our pride. Those are the books I associate most with our stay in Cassiciacum. I turned David's prayers into my own, reciting them aloud, as though in hope that all humanity would respond to their message.

Of course, I was as yet a novice in God's love, a newly arrived foreigner in the state of grace, as was Alipius. But my mother remained with us, a woman of mature faith, with the patience that comes with age, the gentle understanding of a mother, and the devotion of a true Christian. As we pursued our catechetical studies, slowly being instructed in the faith, she was our constant support and encourager.

I also found myself being opened up to the Holy Spirit. It was true I had received salvation. God had sent his Son to die for sin, raised him from the dead, and exalted him to glory . . . from whence, the Scripture says, "he would pour upon us the Comforter, the Spirit of truth." That had happened, the Spirit had been given, but I was not aware of him. I was forgiven, but I did not yet have perfect peace, partly because I was anxious about those I had in the past led into sin and partly for the recollection of my own past sin.

But there, in the country house of Verecundus, the Holy Spirit began to do his sweet work and to bring joy to my heart. Yet it was through pain that I came closest to him.

It came on me suddenly, a most terrible toothache, such as I had never experienced before. It was so acute that it made me speechless. At that time, tortured with the pain, it came to me to call on all my Christian friends to pray for my healing to the God of all health. I wrote my request on wax letters, which I gave to them so they could join me in prayer. And the moment we bowed our knees to pray— yes, immediately—the pain simply disappeared. I was awestruck. What kind of pain had that been? Where had it come from? By what power had it been taken away instantly?

But deep within me it spoke the reassurance I needed. God's will was being done in me. My heart lifted up to him in praise and joy, rooted in faith.

God's Mercy in Baptism

At the end of the grape harvest, when the new term was due to begin in Milan, I wrote to let my students' parents know that I would not be returning to teaching. I also wrote to Bishop Ambrose, telling him of my former errors and present commitment, and asking him which books he would recommend that I read in order to grow in grace. He suggested the prophet Isaiah, I imagine because he speaks most clearly of the coming gospel and God's purpose for the Gentiles. However, when I started the book I found it difficult and obscure, and put it aside, intending to tackle it later when I was better instructed in the Word of God.

The time had now come for my name to be handed in for baptism, so we left the country and made our way back to Milan. Two others were to be baptized with me, to my great joy in both cases.

The first was, of course, Alipius, who was now a marvelous, humble, and believing Christian. The second was my son, Adeodatus—and what a miracle of God's generosity that was. He was now fifteen, the child of my immoral association, but a young man of great gifts, intelligence, and spiritual maturity. That was little thanks to me, I am afraid, for all I gave him was the sin out of which he was begotten. That he was brought up in the fear of the Lord was entirely of God's grace, who led us both to it even when we were ourselves blind to the truth.

It was a great joy, soon after his baptism, to write a book with him, a kind of dialogue between us called "About the Master." God knows that every word in that book which is put into my son's mouth he did in fact speak, showing at only sixteen an almost miraculous insight into truth. He died as a young man, in earthly terms unfulfilled; but I have great confidence that he is now fulfilled in heaven.

At our baptism the three of us stood together, because in the realm of grace we were all the same age, newborn babies. Immediately all anxiety about my former life and its sins was taken away, and in the following days I experienced an indescribable joy as I went more deeply into God's marvelous plan of salvation.

An Occasion for Celebration

Often when hymns and psalms were being sung in church I would break into tears of joy, both at the sweetness of the singing and also at the marvelous truths contained in the words.

The church at Milan, which we joined, was in any case in a mood of celebration and praise. About a year before, Justina, mother of the young emperor Valentinian, had taken up the Arian heresy and set out to try to remove Bishop Ambrose, who, of course, entirely rejected the false Arian teachings about the nature of Christ. The congregation would take turns guarding the church and its precincts, fearing that her servants would try to do harm to the bishop or arrest him. My mother, with others, prayed literally day and night that the enemy would be restrained.

Actually it was during that time that the church in Milan first began to use hymns and psalms in its services, which up to then had been done only in the eastern church. They were brought in to provide some relief during the lengthy vigils of prayer, but were retained afterward, and eventually the practice was taken up by almost every congregation throughout the rest of the world.

The church was delivered from that time of anxiety in a most remarkable way. The Lord showed Ambrose in a vision the place where the bodies of two martyrs, Gervasius and Protasius, had been hidden many years before. When the secret tomb was found and opened, it became clear that God had preserved the two bodies from corruption. Ambrose arranged for them to be moved and buried with due honor in the church. It was while the procession was on its way that a remarkable miracle occurred. A blind man, someone very well known in the city, a man who had been blind many years, asked his guide to lead him to the procession and then got permission to touch the coffin of the martyrs with his handkerchief. When he had done that, and put the handkerchief to his eyes, he shouted out that he could see—a fact soon evident to the entire crowd.

The result was that the whole city was moved to amazement, and Justina herself, although not going so far as to abandon her heresy completely and join herself to the church, nevertheless did abandon her persecution of the bishop.

I suppose it was the memory of events like those, which happened before my conversion, but about which I had known—without recognizing them as signs and confirmations of the faith—that made me weep during the singing of the hymns. It was partly regret, but mostly joy that now at last I was breathing in Your grace and love, O Lord, insofar as one can breathe it purely in this house of clay.

The Death of My Mother

We were joined in our small household by a young man from my hometown, Euodius, who had been converted and baptized just before us. He, too, intended to follow a rule of life, and together we determined to go back to Carthage and try to find ways of serving the Lord there.

We began with the long overland journey, finally arriving at Ostia, at the mouth of the Tiber River, where we decided to spend a little while preparing ourselves for the sea trip.

One day in the house at Ostia my mother and I were standing in a window looking over the garden. As sometimes happens, we embarked on a profound conversation. Its topic was eternal life, the life of the saints in heaven.

As we spoke, our conversation soared to remarkable heights, even, in a kind of irresistible progress, above the usual limitations of the human mind. We talked on, admiring the wonder of God's acts, and then turned inward, probing into our own souls to see there, too, the hand of God at work. We became aware, intensely aware, of the *present:* not what has been in the past, nor what shall be hereafter, but what *is*, as God himself is.

For a time our conversation left human language behind. I truly believe we tasted, in some small way, eternity itself. Then we sighed and returned to the sound of everyday words, with all the limitations they necessarily have. But in those words we tried to recapture our experience. It seemed to us that eternity is the state where all the tumult of the world is silent, every human tongue still, every human thought set aside or bypassed, all dreams and imaginations and signs and symbols discarded—not through human agents, written words, voice of angel or parable, but rather God himself is making all things known.

Beside that eternal reality, all the joys of earth, even the purest and holiest ones, fade into insignificance. Such an experience gives to his people for the rest of eternity an ecstasy that had been ours for a brief moment of understanding. Does not this fulfill the invitation, "Enter into the joy of the Lord"? But can such a thing happen while we still reside in mortal flesh? Surely it must await that time when we shall rise, changed, "in the twinkling of an eye," into the life of the resurrection.

So we spoke, perhaps not precisely in those words. But God knows that we entered that day into a shared experience that made this life itself seem inferior, and which we described in words like those.

When the moment was over, my mother spoke.

"Augustine, my son, as far as I am concerned, I no longer find any delight in this life. In fact, I don't know what there is left for me to do on earth, nor even why God keeps me here, now that all my earthly hopes are fulfilled. The only thing that made me want to go on living a little while longer was the hope of seeing you become a true Christian before I died. Now God has not only granted that, but more—because I see you turning aside from earthly ambitions and giving yourself wholly to his service. So why should I go on living?"

I cannot remember how I replied, but within five days or so she became ill with a fever. It was so serious that for a while she lapsed into unconsciousness, and we all ran to her bedside. Soon she revived, and seeing myself and my brother Navigius at her side, she first asked us, "Where was I?" and then, fixing her eyes on us, said, "You will bury your mother here."

I was silent, but my brother said something to the effect that he hoped my mother would have the happiness of dying and being buried in her home country. My mother looked at him anxiously and then said, "Lay this body wherever you wish, and don't have any anxiety about it. All I ask is that you remember me in the sacrament, wherever you are." She then fell silent, being very weak and increasingly ill.

For me, however, that brief conversation was a matter for praise. I knew how much, over the years, my mother had worried about her burial arrangements. She had obtained and prepared a place alongside her husband's grave, and had always hoped that, at the end of our distant journeys in Italy, God would grant that her earthly remains should join his in the soil of Tagaste, in North Africa.

I do not know when she abandoned that somewhat superstitious hope, but some time later a friend of hers in Ostia told me that one day they had discussed the matter together. The friend suggested that she must be afraid of dying and being buried so far from her homeland. My mother replied, "Nowhere is far from God. I'm not the least bit worried that he won't know well enough on the day of judgment where to find my body and raise it to new life."

She was ill a little over a week. Then, at the age of fifty-six—when I was thirty-three—God released her holy soul from the prison of her weak and weary body.

Grieving and Believing

When my mother died, I bent over her and closed her eyes. At once an indescribable wave of sorrow flooded my heart and overflowed into tears. As her life slipped away, my son Adeodatus, who was standing by the bed, broke into a loud lamentation, but I and the others quieted him, and soon he too was composed. I repressed my tears, and even at the funeral we did not encourage demonstrations of inconsolable sadness, such as wailing or screaming with grief. We considered such things inappropriate for those who do not think of death as the end of everything and thus a time of abject loss. After all, my mother had not died unhappily. In one sense, she had not died at all, because we all knew that her true faith would bring her to eternal life.

What hurt me inwardly (more than I was prepared to show) was the sudden breaking off of our marvelously close and intimate relationship, the end of something precious and unique to us. She had called me her "good son," but how much better was she a mother to me, and how much I valued all she had done for me over the years.

After she died, when Adeodatus was calmed, Euodius began to sing the psalm, "I will sing unto You, O Lord, of mercy and judgment," and all the household joined us, including many of the believers, and while others were discussing the funeral arrangements I spoke a word to those who had gathered. I think the neighbors were rather surprised, even concluding that I lacked a proper sense of grief. But I knew what was in my heart, even though my face did not betray it.

Indeed, when my mother's body was carried out, I followed it without tears—not even at the eucharist near the grave, which was the custom there. But I was desperately sad inwardly, and I begged the Lord to take away my grief, which I felt to be a denial of our faith.

I remember hearing somewhere that the Greeks believed that a bath helped to draw grief from the mind, but it did not help me. However, soon after bathing I fell asleep—and when I woke, the edge had gone from my grief. As I lay in bed, a verse of one of Ambrose's hymns came to my mind and helped to console me:

> O Lord who made the earth we love
> And set the sun and moon above,
> You fill the passing day with light
> But shade our eyes to sleep by night;

Sleep which restores our body's powers
For labor in the daylight hours,
And calms our overburdened mind
Of every care which it may find.

I began to remember my mother as she used to be in my childhood: so devout a Christian, so gentle and caring a parent. Then, at last and unbidden, the tears began to come. All the tears I had repressed were suddenly given permission, as it were, to flow. They were wept only for God's ears, and for one hour, but I cannot and do not count them sinful or unfaithful.

Now, looking back, I can still find tears at her memory, but they are tears of a different kind. Of course I still remember her holy life and strong faith, but I must also recall that she, like every one of us, was a sinner, and that her only hope of heaven was through the forgiveness won for us on the Cross by the Son of God himself, who now sits at the Father's right hand and "ever makes intercession for us."

Her only hope was in that perfect sacrifice, by which "the indictment of our sins is blotted out" and our enemy Satan is trodden under foot, and through which we are "more than conquerors." To the sacrament of our redemption she clung fast all her life by the bonds of faith. May nothing ever stand between her and God's love. Indeed, I believe God has already answered that prayer for her. My mother would not say she had never sinned; but she would and did say that her sins were all forgiven for his sake.

So she rests in peace with her husband Patricius, whom she won for the Lord. These two, my parents in this fleeting life, my brother and sister in the church, my fellow citizens in the New Jerusalem.

PART VII

Teacher and Preacher

This section of the book contains a small selection, a sample, of the vast body of writings on the Christian life, on spirituality, on major questions of the faith, that Augustine left us.

We have already seen how important the Psalms were to him at one stage in his life. That interest is reflected here as well, as are a number of the questions he had wrestled with during the years of his pilgrimage to faith.

What emerges most of all, however, is the heart of the pastor and teacher. Augustine always *applied* the truths of the Bible—not always, one has to admit, according to the best principles of Bible interpretation as we know them today. But he used his biblical understanding to open up issues, to warn, rebuke, encourage, and inspire in a way that few modern preachers and writers can equal. The bishop of Hippo, who died in A.D. 430, speaks to us today.

The Dangers of Gossip

One of the great examples set me by my mother was her concern to use speech and conversation to make peace rather than destroy it.

She won her mother-in-law over by refusing to speak ill of her even when she was being constantly criticized—largely, she later discovered, through malicious rumors circulated by some of the servants. Eventually patience and a gentle tongue won her over.

It was my mother's rule of life to report to other people only what might help reconcile them to their enemies, and never what would serve to stir up strife. If she spoke separately to two people who were in dispute, she would tell the one only positive and helpful things the other had said. It may seem a tiny virtue. My experience, however, is that most people in such circumstances, perhaps as one of the consequences of fallen human nature, tend to pass on the most inflammatory parts of what they have heard—and even to embellish them.

There is no way to peace, as it has been said; rather, peace is the way.

It Is Not *What* But *How* We Know That Matters

Lord, You are not pleased with someone simply because that person is knowledgeable. In fact, it would be possible for one to know everything there is to know in the whole wide world, except for knowing You, and consequently know nothing. Just as another person could live in blissful ignorance of the great sum of human knowledge, *but know You*, and be both happy and content.

After all, who is better placed—the person who owns a tree and gives You thanks for all the good things it provides; or the one who owns a similar tree and knows its weight and dimensions down to the least leaf, but does not realize that You are its Creator and that it is through You that he or she has the use of it? In essence, the latter person is ignorant, though full of facts, and the former person wise, though a bit short on details.

So in general we can say that the most important knowledge is knowledge of You, O Lord. A person who has that, as Paul said, "possesses nothing yet owns everything." We may not know the course of the Great Bear through the sky, we may not be able to analyze chemical elements nor measure continents, but we can know You, our Creator and God, who plots the courses of the stars, creates the elements, and shapes the land and sky and sea. Better to know the Planner than the Plan.

Obeying God and Caesar

There is obviously a difference between the law of man and the law of God. Human law is based on a tremendous variety of customs and practices, whereas God's law is consistent and absolute.

That doesn't mean, of course, that we can disregard human laws, the laws of our state and government, with impunity. A law that is ratified by the constitution of a city or nation is the will of the whole body, and it is unacceptable that individuals should set themselves against the community of which they are only a part.

So Christians respect their nation's laws, but they do not give them precedence over the law of God. When God commands anything, it must be done. Yes, it must be done even if it is against the rules or customs of our society, even if it is completely without precedent. If God commands us to do something that we have stopped doing for one reason or another, then we must take it up again. If God commands something to be set up that doesn't at present exist, then we must set it up.

The reason is simple. It is completely lawful for an earthly ruler to decree something that is totally new, and his subjects are bound to obey it unless it is completely against the common good—and as in general we are agreed that an ordered society depends on our obedience to the law, it is unlikely that an individual could justify opposing it. So if we give that kind of unqualified obedience to law made and enforced by human beings, how much more should we unhesitatingly obey everything that God commands? In the hierarchy of human society the greater power (for instance, the state) receives obedience from the lesser (for instance, the individual). As God's power is infinite, he can claim obedience from every creature—and no argument of personal preference or general good carries any weight at all against that.

The Language of the Heart

At school I had to learn Greek, and I hated it. People told me how wonderful the stories of Homer were, but to be honest I didn't enjoy them. I dare say the plots were gripping, the dialogue witty and subtle, but it was all wasted on me. It is hard to enjoy a book when every sentence represents an obstacle course and you are spending more time in the dictionary than you are on the story. And it doesn't help when a teacher is standing over you with a ruler, giving you a smart rap every time you get it wrong.

Of course, there was a time when I had to learn Latin, too. But that was easy. No one stood over me. There was no pressure or compulsion. My nurses spoke it to me as they bathed me or changed my clothes. My parents chattered in it at the dinner table. When I did something clever, it was in the words of Latin that they praised me. When someone made me laugh, the joke was in that familiar tongue.

So naturally, as time went on, when I wanted to say something or praise someone or make them laugh, I did it in Latin—probably getting it quite wrong at first, but nobody minded. It was *my* language, the language of the heart, and I learned it from talkers, not teachers. The moral of that seems to be that curiosity, freedom, and enjoyment are better ways of learning than necessity, fear, or compulsion.

Then, I ask myself, is this true in the spiritual realm? Do I learn the ways of God best by fear, duty, and compulsion? Or by freedom and joy, simply being at home in my Father's house? Can I "pick up" the language of the Spirit as I picked up my mother tongue?

I decided that the answer is No. The things of the Spirit do not come naturally, like a mother tongue, to fallen people. Delight and joy and freedom will indeed help me to learn, but behind them there does need to be—however much we may wish it were not so—the divine compulsion, the pressure of the Holy Spirit, the restraint of God's firm though loving discipline. Left to ourselves, who knows where "freedom and delight" might take us?

What Is God Like?

"Who is Lord beside our Lord? Who is God beside our God?" Yet we long to know what You are like, to understand how it can be that You combine so many apparently conflicting qualities. You are supreme over all, infinitely powerful, utterly merciful, and yet perfectly just. You are able to hide Yourself from us and yet be with us all the time. You are the source of beauty and yet also of raw energy. You are totally reliable and yet we cannot begin to comprehend You. You never change, yet You are the agent of change in everything You have made. Because You are eternal You are neither young nor old, yet You make all things new. And all the while, quietly and unnoticed, You are drawing the proud along the pathway to decay. You are restlessly active and yet the source of rest. You sustain, fill, protect, create, nourish, and perfect all that is.

You love perfectly, but without allowing that love to become an obsession, as we do. You are described as "jealous," but are without hatred or anxiety. You are said to be "angry," but are without sin or distortion. You change Your actions without changing Your purposes.

You have everything, and yet You are pleased to see things flourish. You are in no sense greedy, yet You expect us to give You our talents and our gifts. You owe us nothing, yet You pay off all our debts of failure and sin.

This God of my life, my holy joy. What can I do but praise him?

God and the Passing of Time

For all good things come from You, O Lord, and the whole course of my salvation comes from my God.

Your blessings to me began long, long before I could know what they were and where they came from. As a newborn baby, all I knew was how to suck and be content with the result. Later I began to laugh, and, very slowly, by degrees, to discover where I was. But when I wanted to explain my wishes to those around me—parents, nursemaids, and so on—I found I couldn't. I knew what I wanted, but I couldn't communicate with them nor they with me. Consequently, getting very frustrated, I waved my arms, cried, and eventually when none of that succeeded, went into a red-faced rage.

Now that wasn't exceptional, by any means. Ordinary, day-to-day experience tells us that such behavior is common to all babies, but eventually they learn to communicate, and the period of frustration passes.

Yet even as a baby I had a being and a life and desperately wanted to find some way of expressing myself to others. That seems reasonable for a being made in Your image, Lord. You are Yourself Being and Life, and in Your love You have expressed Yourself to us. You have communicated that being and life to Your creatures.

"Your years do not fail ... You are still the same." So all Your years are like this present day. We move on from infancy through childhood to each succeeding age, to the point where we are now. But tomorrow, with whatever lies ahead, and yesterday, with all that is past, are contained within this present day of Yours, neither future nor past, but eternally present.

Worthy to Be Praised

You are great, O Lord, and worthy to be praised: Your power is great, and Your wisdom endless.

As well as the hosts of heaven, human beings also long to praise You—yes, even we, born to die and burdened with the knowledge of it. We, in our petty pride of life, even we long to praise You. By Your own design, praising You gives us a strange, inexplicable joy because You have made us for Yourself, and our hearts are restless until they rest in You.

So, Lord, I have two questions. Which should come first—to turn to You for forgiveness or to praise You for it? And then again, which should be first—to know You or to turn to You?

After all, no one is going to turn to someone they don't know. They will be just as likely to turn to someone or something else. On the other hand, perhaps Your intention is that as we turn to You, as we call to You for help, You will make Yourself known to us. As the apostle Paul wrote, "How shall they call upon him in whom they have not believed? And how shall they believe without a preacher?" But the psalmist stated the other case: "Those who seek the Lord shall praise him . . . Those who seek the Lord shall find him." And, of course, those who find him shall praise him.

So what shall I do? I shall seek You, Lord, by turning to You and calling for Your help. But I shall turn to You in faith, because in fact the truth about You has been preached to me. It is my faith—given by You in the Son of Man, Jesus, and shown to me by the ministry of a faithful preacher—that turns to You and calls to You for help. Faith speaks to faith.

Seeing and Believing

Christians believe that, in some sense of the words, we can "see" God. We do not think of this, of course, as seeing with our physical eyesight. Nor do we think of it in that other common use of seeing, when we see things in our imagination or understand our actions, intentions, or desires with our mind. "I see" can cover all of those. But it cannot really be used of God, because we do not see him with our eyes, cannot really imagine what he is like, and cannot comprehend him with our minds. So eye, imagination, and intellect are not the means by which we can be said to see God.

Yet Scripture says that the pure in heart shall see God (Matthew 5:8). How can that be? The Scripture cannot lead us astray.

In fact, we often believe things that we have not seen and cannot imagine: that Rome was founded by Romulus, or Constantinople by Constantine; that our parents conceived us, and that we have different and distant ancestors. Now we cannot know these things by sight (we were not around when they happened) nor by our mental reasoning or insight. We have to accept them on the testimony of someone else.

That someone must, of course, be seen by us as trustworthy, and his testimony must not contradict what we have learned from other sources, already accepted as trustworthy. So things about God that we are shown or told by the testimony of others cannot be accepted if they contradict the Bible.

So what is the connection between seeing and believing? Is the former what we do with something that is present and the latter what we do with something that is absent?

But it is not that simple. After all, I can see with my physical eyes, and hear with my physical ears, someone who is actually present with me as he tries to persuade me to do something. Whether I actually do what he wants or not depends not on his physical presence, nor on my physical awareness of it, but on whether I believe him or not.

And that, in turn, depends on whether the authority by which he urges me to do something seems trustworthy. This is why we believe what the Bible tells us about the creation, or about the resurrection of Jesus, even though we have not seen them with our eyes. We believe the witness to be trustworthy.

So knowledge consists of things seen and things believed. Of the things we see (or have seen in the past) we are our own witnesses. But where the things we believe are concerned, we depend on the witness of others whom we judge to be trustworthy. So it is not unreasonable to argue that belief of that kind is not inferior to seeing, because, in a way, we see with our mental sight—and on appropriate evidence—what we come to believe firmly. Experience may support it, logic may back it up, and it is based on the evidence of those we judge to be totally reliable. We can see things with our eyes and get them quite wrong. We can believe with our minds what we cannot possibly see, and get it right.

As the apostle Peter says, "Though you have never seen him, yet I know that you love him"; and as the Lord himself said, "Blessed are those *who have not seen* but have believed."

The Pure in Heart See God

In the Resurrection we shall receive spiritual bodies. This corruptible, mortal body will put on incorruption and immortality: "We shall be changed," as Paul says. And in that new and spiritual body we shall see God.

Now that raises a question at once. We see with our eyes. Does this mean that in heaven we shall have bodies like our earthly ones, complete with physical eyes? Or is there some other way of seeing that does not require a bodily organ to achieve it?

We are told in Scripture that God the Father sees the Son and that, at the dawn of creation, he saw the light and the skies and the sea and the dry land. Indeed, "God *saw* all the things that he had made and behold they were very good."

But God is spirit. We do not believe him to have a body or to be limited by a physical form. So vision is not attributable only or exclusively to bodies. There must be a way of seeing that is consistent with pure spiritual being. Indeed, all through the Bible that kind of spiritual vision is described, and is regarded as superior to ordinary physical sight. After all, the prophets were called "see-ers."

Having said that, we must be careful not to fall into the opposite error, which is to say that through the resurrection the body not only puts off its mortal and corruptible state, but also the very state of being a body at all, so that in heaven we are *only* spirits. That would be to deny the immortality of the body, which is clearly taught in Scripture. What Paul said was that our bodies at the Resurrection will be *changed*, not cease to exist at all. The Lord Jesus, who is the pattern or prototype of our resurrection, is said to "see the Father" in heaven.

But more important than such questions, to be honest, is this one: What are the conditions to be fulfilled for *us* to see God in heaven? The answer is given us by the Lord himself: "Blessed are *the pure in heart:* They shall see God."

You know how much I admire Bishop Ambrose, because through him the Lord freed me from error and led me to salvation and baptism. I particularly like some words he wrote on this subject—not just because of my personal admiration for him, but because they are based on the truth of Scripture itself.

He wrote, "Even in the resurrection itself it is not easy to see God, except for those who are pure of heart. For the Lord listed many virtuous people who were to be blessed by God, but only the pure in heart would be able to see him."

If, then, only the pure in heart see God, it suggests there are others who will not see him: the unworthy, the impure, and those who do not have a genuine desire to see him.

But the pure in heart *will* see him, and not just at that day of resurrection. They will see him when he comes to them and makes his dwelling in their hearts, here and now.

Let us therefore cleanse our hearts and make room for him, so that he may open our eyes and we may see his glory.

The Presence of God

Although Almighty God is wholly present everywhere, he does not dwell in everyone. And those in whom he dwells he does not necessarily fill.

It is a truth about God's nature that he fills the entire universe—not by his bulk, as though half of God filled one half and the other half of him the rest of creation, but by the quality of his being. He is the power that sustains it, wholly present in every part of it. As God says through the prophet, "I fill heaven and earth." There is nowhere to go where he is not. "Where can I go from your Spirit, and where can I hide from your presence?"

So isn't it remarkable that the God who fills every part of the universe can be excluded from human hearts that he has made? The apostle Paul speaks of those who "do not have the Spirit of

Christ" (Romans 8:9), and, because we believe that the Holy Trinity cannot be divided, it is not possible that God the Father would be present in someone in whom the Holy Spirit does not dwell.

It seems to follow, then, that God is everywhere by the presence of his divine nature, but he is *not* present in every person by the grace of his indwelling. By unbelief and sin we can exclude the Lord of creation from the heart of his creature.

But just as God does not dwell within everyone, so he does not equally fill everyone in whom he does dwell. Otherwise, why should Elisha pray twice for the Spirit of God to be in him that was in Elijah? And how else can we explain that some Christians are clearly holier than others, unless God is dwelling more completely in them?

This raises a further question. If God is wholly present everywhere in his creation, how can it be that he is more or less present in some of his creatures (and not present in some of them at all)?

The answer lies in the capacity of things to receive him, not in his willingness to fill them. The universe, which he made and designated "very good," has the capacity to receive him, so he fills every part of it with his presence and power. But the human spirit, through rebellion and sin, has become wholly *unlike* him, and, apart from forgiveness and grace, lacks the capacity to receive him. If blind eyes cannot receive the light of the sun, it is not the sun's fault. It shines everywhere, but not everything has the capacity to receive its light. So it is with God. If a person, through sin and unbelief, receives less of him, it does not lessen him in any way. God in himself is whole and complete, and does not need to find a dwelling place in human hearts. Our hearts need *him*, as the means of life and health.

God is eternally reliable, able to be present completely in each individual person. Although each believer may possess him in different degree, according to each one's varied capacities—some more, some less—yet by the grace of his goodness he builds them all up as his most precious temple, the place of his perfect dwelling.

In Search of the Land of the Happy Life

If we think of people as travelers at sea, navigating their boats according to different principles of life, we can see at least three types. There are those who set out oblivious of the conditions and end up a little way out to sea, becalmed but in a state of tranquility. They have not expended much effort getting there, but are happy to advise others to join them.

A second group, in contrast, misled by the apparent calm of the sea, strike out for the deeps and get carried far away from their homeland. If some attractive current or wind suddenly carries them along, they happily go with it, even accepting storms and tempests as enjoyable problems. Occasionally, however, a particularly severe setback will drive them at long last to consult their charts, and perhaps even to set course for that safe harbor that they so imprudently left long ago.

The third group consists of those who, having launched out onto the sea in their youth, remember the reliable beacons of their homeland and, fixing their compasses on them, make straight for their home port, despite all distractions of weather or fortune. It is the memory of home that draws them, not the wisdom of experience.

In fact, all of us are really travelers in search of the land of the happy life, the City of God. What we need to know most of all is that blocking the harbor to that land is a mountainous rock rising out of the sea. It should be seriously feared and carefully avoided.

True, it has a very pleasant look about it and is bathed in a deceptively beautiful light. Often those seeking the land of the happy life are foolish enough to think that this mountainous island is preferable to the land itself, thereby losing their ambition to complete the journey. Some are even attracted to leave the land and make for the rock, captivated by its height and by the way it enables them to look down on others. The main danger of this island is that it presents itself as an attractive alternative to seekers who are heading for the happy life but have not yet landed there, and therefore it draws them astray.

All who seek true knowledge of themselves and of God should fear that mountainous island, which is *pride* and *empty glory*. For underneath its ground-crust there is nothing substantial or solid. It collapses under one's feet and swallows up all those who walk on it, consuming them on the threshold of that gleaming and happy land that they had distantly seen but foolishly failed to enter.

A Song of Steps:
A Meditation on
Psalm 120

This psalm is called a Song of Ascents—a song sung as people climbed upward, step by step, toward the temple. It is a psalm about spiritual progress: progress *upward* from the valley of tears toward the place of blessing. Let us resolve to ascend in heart, since Christ himself descended to earth so that we might ascend to heaven.

We can see among the people of God how true it is that some ascend progressing upward toward God, and some descend, falling back into sin and failure. Those who ascend are those who progress toward spiritual understanding. Those who fall back are those who are satisfied with "milk" when they should be taking spiritual food. It is often fear that holds us back, and it is often wisdom that draws us higher.

So let us imagine ourselves to be the one who is longing to ascend. Where will this ascent take place? In the heart. From where will we begin our ascent? From humility, the valley of tears. And where will we ascend to? To the place described in this psalm as "the place he has appointed."

Now as soon as a Christian sets out seriously to advance in holiness, to "ascend to the place God has appointed," that person becomes the object of enemy attack, and especially of enemy tongues. Anyone who has never yet experienced such an attack has not yet seriously taken the upward path, and those who are not experiencing it now are not themselves on the way.

But once let Christian men and women set their minds to ascend, to despise worldly and passing values, to put God first and rate pleasure and popularity low, then see how ridicule and criticism are drawn to them. It is not only enemies who attack them. Perhaps more distressing are the negative comments of friends who purport to give them good advice, because to give advice should be an activity of blessing, to help a person toward salvation, whereas these advisers set out to turn their friends away from what is spiritually healthy.

Attacks of this kind, whether from friends or enemies, are called "deceitful tongues" in the Bible. So, before the ascent begins, the psalmist asks for God's help to counter those attacks: "Lord, I called to You in my troubles and You answered me." Why did God answer? To set him on the upward path, to put his feet on the steps that lead higher, to the "place he has appointed." And what was the petition that God answered? "Lord, deliver my soul from unjust lips and from treacherous tongues." It is these tongues that will deter us from the upward climb—these deceitful, flattering, misleading voices. Only God, who calls us higher, can deliver us from them.

Sharp Arrows of Love: A Meditation on Psalm 120:4

What is God's answer to treacherous tongues, to deceitful enemies and unhelpful friends? He himself tells us, "The arrows of the powerful are sharp, like desolating coals." *Desolating* here could equally well be translated "laying waste." The words have similar meaning, because to lay something to waste is to bring desolation.

Let us first consider what these "arrows" are that are God's means of deliverance from treacherous tongues. "The sharp arrows of the powerful" are the words of God. When they are shot, they penetrate right into the heart—but not to bring death, like an ordinary arrow, but to bring love and life. The Lord knows how to fire arrows of love, and no one can shoot a better arrow of love than those who fire the arrow of God's Word. They pierce the heart of the person who loves them, but only to help them love better; and they pierce the heart of the one whose love grows cold in order to fan it back into a blaze.

So words are arrows, but what are these "desolating coals"? They are the burning coals that lay waste our earthly thoughts, clearing away the ground where all those insidious, negative ideas proposed by the treacherous tongues have taken root. You know the sort of thing. God has called us to do something, but we begin to look at and listen to those misleading voices. What makes you think you can do it? And why is it that this other Christian is so much stronger than you? How can this sick man or that impoverished woman achieve so readily what you find so hard? So the Christian is pierced to the heart by God's command, totally discouraged by his or her own hurt pride and human desire to succeed and be well thought of.

It is at this point that the hot coals are applied, burning away the unhealthy vegetation that has overrun the soul—the vegetation of worldly thoughts and ambitions—and clearing the ground so that

God can build his temple there. The desolating coals, then, are sent to destroy what has been planted in our hearts by evil.

But coals can be "live." An extinguished coal is called a dead coal, and a glowing one a live coal. So a coal can also be a picture of conversion: of someone who was dead, but is kindled into life by being put alongside a burning coal. The results are sometimes surprising. A drunkard, a villain, a man addicted to the games of the arena, a swindler, can become a committed Christian, fervently serving the Lord, glowing like a live coal.

The Tents of Kedar: A Meditation on Psalm 120:5

The psalmist now utters a sad cry. "My soul has wandered far, I have dwelt among the tents of Kedar."

All Christians understand something of this dilemma, for there is a sense in which we live on the earth as "strangers and exiles." We cry out to God "from the ends of the earth." But the exile is not one of fulfillment, but of sorrow. "Alas, my sojourning has become far off."

We find ourselves among "the tents of Kedar." What are they? The word *Kedar* means "darkness," and the tents of Kedar are the tents of Ishmael, the company of those who offer God a carnal, unspiritual, legalistic worship. The psalmist is trapped in a place of spiritual dryness and darkness: "I have dwelt among the tents of Kedar."

His experience there is even more bitter: "With those who hate peace, I was peaceful, and when I spoke to them, they attacked me without cause."

Who hates peace? Surely the person who destroys unity. Unity is peace. Disunity breaks peace. The Lord's will for the church is its peace and unity, and he will in the end judge those who destroy it. But for the present, in the interest of peace, we may be called to "dwell among" them, until that day when God separates the good from the evil and brings only pure grain into the heavenly granaries. So we are peaceful among those who hate peace. These are the words of those who are truly Christ's but are called to live in the midst of chaff.

But still we must bear our witness: Love peace, love Christ—to love peace is to love Christ. Paul tells us that Christ is our peace because he made a unity of two conflicting peoples, "making the two one" (Ephesians 2:14). So we must say to those who claim to be Christ's but hate peace, "Why, if Christ is our peace because he has reunited two peoples into one, do you try to make of one people two? How can you be peacemakers by causing division?" To say this to those who hate peace is to "be peaceful." But when we do say that, these enemies of peace "attack us without cause."

The Guard Who Never Sleeps: A Meditation on Psalm 121

As he ascends step by step in his spiritual pilgrimage to the temple of God, the psalmist prays, "Do not allow my foot to be moved."

Who "moves" our feet? Who moved Adam's feet in Eden, to turn him out of paradise? Surely the same Enemy who moves our feet from the safe path. But, first of all, what moved the foot of the angel who fell, with such appalling consequences? We are told in Scripture that he fell *by pride*. Pride turns our steps in the wrong direction, away from God and goodness, away from faith. Faith and trust are the enemies of pride, because faith is an expression of humility: "Under the shadow of Your wings they shall put their trust."

The psalmist expresses his prayer simply: "Do not allow my foot to be moved." God's answer is also simple: "Do not let your guardian fall asleep." If you do not wish to stumble and fall on the upward path, then see that the one who looks after you does not fall asleep. See that he is alert, guarding your every step. Then you will not fall; your foot will not be moved.

But we might reply, "It's not in our power to insure that our keeper never falls asleep. Of course we don't want our guard to sleep on the task, but how can we prevent it?"

The answer surely is "By choosing the right guardian." Choose a keeper who never sleeps. But is there such a person? Surely everyone has to sleep at some time. The answer is given in the psalm. "Israel's keeper" never sleeps. "He who guards Israel shall neither slumber nor sleep." God does not sleep, he is never off duty, he never rests from his eternal task of guarding and guiding his people.

In his passion the Lord Jesus passed from death to life, opening a way for us who believe in him also to pass from death to life. Many people believe that Christ died: the heathen do, the Jews do, many a wicked person does. Christian faith is distinguished by believing that Christ *rose* from the dead. "Christ, being risen from the dead, dies no more. Death no longer has any power over him."

Death is the ultimate picture of sleep, the final conqueror of mortal beings. If you wish to choose a guard who never sleeps, then choose one who cannot die. Every human being sleeps, and every human being dies. So do not put your confidence in any mortal, but in the Lord Jesus who has conquered death and, like the Father, "never sleeps." "The Lord will guard you"—not a man, who sleeps, slumbers, and dies, but the Lord of life and conqueror of death. He will watch your every step as you climb the hill of the Lord.

Going Out and Coming In: A Meditation on Psalm 121:8

"The Lord watch over your coming and going, from this time even for ever more." Let us reflect for a moment on this coming and going. What are they?

I would suggest that for us the *coming* is temptation; and victory over it is the *going*. The Lord, like the potter, places clay vessels in the kiln of testing, and when they are fired, he takes them out. When the potter puts them in, he is not sure of their quality, but he is when he takes them out. The Lord, on the other hand, "knows those who are his," those who will not crack under the heat—and it is the humble ones who best survive the test.

Indeed, in every temptation it is humility that guards us. We climb up from the valley of tears singing the Song of Ascent, and as we do the Lord watches over us to see that we enter his temple safely. "He is faithful," as Paul says, "and will not permit us to be tested beyond our endurance." So the Lord watches over our coming into the place of testing and our going out from it in victory.

Part of that *watching over*, where coming in is concerned, is to remove from us the trial that is beyond our strength. But he also watches over our going out. "He provides a way out, so that you may be able to bear it."

So let us not trust in our own strength to defend ourselves. Rather, let us trust in the Lord to protect and guard us. He does not slumber or sleep—though once he did sleep the sleep of death for us. But now he is risen, never to die again.

As we make our way up from the valley of tears, let us not dawdle or hang back. There is still some way to go, and laziness and pride will try to suggest other and easier ways of getting there. But we can reject them, and climb on steadily toward our goal—if our trust is in the One who watches over our going out and coming in, who guards our feet, and who shields us from the burning sun of day and the chilling moon of night.

If we trust in ourselves, our foot is already "moved," and if it *is* moved, even though we have a degree of faith, pride will cause us to stumble and fall. The one who walks humbly up from the valley of tears toward the hill of the Lord is the one who prays, "Do not let my foot be moved."

The Heavenly Jerusalem: A Meditation on Psalm 122

This, too, is a Song of Ascent. The psalmist wishes to go up, up to heaven or, as it is put here, up to Jerusalem. "I was glad when they said to me, 'Let us go to the house of the Lord.'" Like a crowd gathering for a pilgrimage to a holy shrine, the worshipers press forward and upward to the great temple in Jerusalem. They run, they hurry. There is excitement and eagerness. So let us be excited at the prospect of joining God's people and going into his house. Let us rejoice with those who have gone there before us, the prophets and apostles who also call to us, "Let us go to the house of the Lord."

"Our feet were standing in your courts, O Jerusalem." In fact, they have not yet arrived, but such is their faith and hope, it is *as though* their feet are already on holy ground. You see, you possess the Lord's house if you faithfully seek it. Those who climb upward should encourage themselves by thinking that they are already there. "Our feet stand in your courts." It makes the climb much easier.

But what "Jerusalem" is this? After all, Jerusalem is the name of an earthly city, one that at this time is in ruins. Why should we long to stand in a ruined and desolate foreign city? But the psalmist, through the Spirit, does not sing of the earthly Jerusalem, built of stones and wood and mortar—the Jerusalem that "kills the prophets and stones those sent to her"—but of the heavenly Jerusalem, the one that Paul called "the mother of us all . . . eternal in the heavens."

This Jerusalem is described here as "being built as a city." When David spoke those words, the city of Jerusalem was already built. The city that was still being built was the new Jerusalem, the one built not with bricks but with living stones (as Peter says), built on the foundation of Jesus Christ. It is a city in the heavens, with a heavenly foundation. Every preacher of the truth helps to cut the stones, but it is the Lord himself who shapes them into his building. If we have faith, then we are part of the building toward which we press. "You are built as living stones . . . You are the temple of God."

That city is marked by one shining quality: "Jerusalem is built as a city that is at unity with itself." All its inhabitants are in unity. Like the Lord who made it, it is always the same, not now one thing and then something else. God is One, and always the same. Christ is One, and always the same. And if we, under the pressure of daily life with all its passing values and changing circumstances, feel that we are variable, inconsistent, then let us remember that if we cannot ascend, *he* descended. He came to us—the one who is "eternally the same"—to make us what we cannot make ourselves.